. . . From induction into the U.S.

. . . To the landing on Utah Beach

. . . From foxhole to foxhole in France and Belgium

. . . To triumph and victory in Germany

. . . As a member of an Infantry Combat Division

One Soldier's Journey

Memoirs of World War II

Written by
James L. Thome, Captain, Infantry
Army of the United States
63rd Infantry Division
79th Infantry Division

© Copyright 2002 James L. Thome and Judith K. Thome. All rights reserved.

No part of this publication may be reproduced, stored in a retrieval system, or transmitted, in any form or by any means, electronic, mechanical, photocopying, recording, or otherwise, without the written prior permission of the author.

Printed in Victoria, Canada

National Library of Canada Cataloguing in Publication

Thome, James L., 1919-
    One soldier's journey / James L. Thome.

Includes bibliographical references.
ISBN 1-55395-084-4

    1. World War, 1939-1945—Personal narratives, American.
I. Title.

D811.T496 2002   940.54'8173   C2002-904355-7

TRAFFORD

This book was published *on-demand* in cooperation with Trafford Publishing.
On-demand publishing is a unique process and service of making a book available for retail sale to the public taking advantage of on-demand manufacturing and Internet marketing.
On-demand publishing includes promotions, retail sales, manufacturing, order fulfilment, accounting and collecting royalties on behalf of the author.

Suite 6E, 2333 Government St., Victoria, B.C. V8T 4P4, CANADA
Phone   250-383-6864   Toll-free   1-888-232-4444 (Canada & US)
Fax   250-383-6804   E-mail   sales@trafford.com
Web site   www.trafford.com   TRAFFORD PUBLISHING IS A DIVISION OF TRAFFORD HOLDINGS LTD.
Trafford Catalogue #02-0798   www.trafford.com/robots/02-0798.html

10   9   8   7   6   5   4   3

Memoirs of a Civilian Drafted to Fight World War II

One Soldier's Journey

Dedication

To my wonderful children who resulted from my miraculous survival – Judith K. Thome, James K. Thome, Janet M. Crowley, Jacqueline A. Wondolowski, and John Francis Thome, and to their devoted and caring mother, Marian A. Thome, who passed away March 6, 1990.

Special Acknowledgments

To my daughter, Judy, for her encouragement, suggestions and prodding that resulted in my story; for her hour upon hour of computer time, correcting, researching, editing and proof reading. To her, my utmost thanks.

To Lee, my wife, who helped me through many difficult physical adversities while writing my memoirs. I couldn't have done it without her.

Thank you both.

And, especially to Mary Greene, for her hour upon hour of computer work, adjusting, revising, editing and correcting, and by so doing, contributed so enormously to its conclusion.

Forward

I had to write these war memoirs not only as an historic record for my family but also as a tribute to all the soldiers who lived or died while serving with me in Company L and who endured the pain, misery and heartbreaks of World War II.

Contents

Dedication

Special Acknowledgments

Forward

Eulogy for A Soldier

Chapter 1
A Nation at War, Grand Rapids, Michigan, January 30, 1942   1

Chapter 2
If It Fits, Camp Custer, Battle Creek, Michigan, February 1942   4

Chapter 3
Secret Passage, Camp Joseph T. Robinson, Little Rock, Arkansas
February 1942 – October 1942   7

Chapter 4
This is the Army, Camp Joseph T. Robinson, Little Rock, Arkansas
February 1942 – October 1942   10

Chapter 5
Corporal to Lieutenant, Camp Joseph T. Robinson, Little Rock, Arkansas
Late October 1942   13

Chapter 6
Nightmare of OCS, Fort Benning – Columbus, Georgia
November 1942 – January 1943   16

Chapter 7
Graduation, Fort Benning, Columbus, Georgia
December 1943 – March 1, 1943   19

Chapter 8
A Wedding and First Assignment, Grand Rapids, Michigan to Fort
McClellan, Anniston, Alabama, March 6, 1943 – May 1943   22

Chapter 9
How It Was, Camp McClellan, Anniston, Alabama
March 1943 – May 1943   25

Chapter 10
On the Move, Camp Blanding, Jacksonville, Florida
May 21, 1943 – August 1943   27

Chapter 11
Here They Come! Camp Van Dorn, McComb, Mississippi
September 23, 1943 – April 19, 1944   29

Chapter 12
Off to War, Camp Van Dorn, McComb, Mississippi, April 18, 1944   32

Chapter 13
Countdown to Battle, Fort George G. Meade, Baltimore, Maryland
April 19, 1944 – May 2, 1944   35

Chapter 14
Out to Sea, Camp Myles Standish and Boston Harbor, Boston, Maine
May 3, 1944 – May 12, 1944   37

Chapter 15
"Ten Shilling Hill", Warminster Barracks – Whitchurch, England
Mid-May 1944 – Mid-June 1944   40

Chapter 16
Crossing the English Channel and Utah Beach, Utah Beach, Normandy,
France, June 15,1944   43

Chapter 17
Hedgerows and Lieutenant B. B. Walker, Normandy, France
Late June 1944 – Mid-July 1944   46

Chapter 18
Hedgerow Country, Lessay, France, Late July 1944   51

Chapter 19
Operation Cobra, Lessay, France, Late July 1944   55

Chapter 20
"Blood and Guts", Avranches, France to the Battle of the Falaise Gap
Late July 1944 – Mid August 14, 1944   59

Chapter 21
Sitting Ducks, Remois, France, Mid August 1944 – September 15, 1944   64

Chapter 22
Combat Fatigue, Foret de Parroy, Luneville, France, September 1944   69

Chapter 23
Despair, Bayon and Saverne, France, October 1944   73

Chapter 24
The Ugly Americans, Strasbourg, Colmar and Mulhouse, France
October 1944 – November 1944   77

Chapter 25
Trench Foot, Bischwiller and Haguenau, France, December 1944   81

Chapter 26
A German Prisoner, Bischwiller and Haguenau, France, December 1944   85

Chapter 27
Horrors of Combat, Wissembourg, France, Mid-December 1944   88

Chapter 28
Battle of the Bulge, Wissembourg, France, Mid-December 1944   91

Chapter 29
Stalemate, Rittershoffen, France, Early to Mid-January 1945   95

Chapter 30
Lieutenant Kilev, Battle of Rittershoffen, France, January 19, 1945   100

Chapter 31
Private Bill Newman, Missing! Tongres, Belgium, February 1945   104

Chapter 32
Operation Flashpoint, Brunssum, Holland, March 1945   109

Chapter 33
Our Turn, Brunssum, Holland, March 23, 1945   113

Chapter 34
On to Berlin! Essen, Germany, Early April 1945   117

Chapter 35
Displaced Prisoners, Bochum and Mulheim, Germany
Mid-April 1945   120

Chapter 36
Mayor of Bochum, Bochum, Germany, April 17, 1945 – April 21, 1945   124

Chapter 37
Camp Lucky Strike and Homeward Bound, Le Havre, France to Camp
Patrick Henry, Newport Beach, Virginia, April 22, 1945 – May 8, 1945   128

Chapter 38
USA! Camp Patrick Henry, Newport News, Virginia, May 1945   132

Chapter 39
Reassignment, Fort Sheridan, Chicago, IL to Fort Sam Houston, Houston,
Texas, May 16, 1945 – July 9, 1945   135

Chapter 40
Atom Bomb, Camp Blanding, Jacksonville, Florida
July 18,1945 – September 16, 1945   139

Chapter 41
Back to Michigan, Camp Blanding, Jacksonville, Florida
August 1945 – September 16, 1945   143

Appendices:

A.   Military Vitae

B.   Miscellaneous items

C.   About the Author

EULOGY FOR A SOLDIER

Author Unknown

Do not stand at my grave and weep.
I am not there, I do not sleep.
I am a thousand winds that blow.
I am a thousand diamond glints on snow.
I am the sunlight on ripened grain.
I am the gentle autumn rain.
When you awaken in the morning's hush,
I am that swift uplifting rush
Of quiet birds in circled flight.
I am the soft stars that shine at night.
Do not stand at my grave and cry.
I am not there, I did not die.

Chapter 1

A Nation at War

Grand Rapids, Michigan
January 30, 1942

When I was twenty-two years, four months and seven days old, I was inducted as a draftee into the United States Army. At that time, I was living at home and working at the Kelvinator Corporation in their inspection department, air-testing refrigerators to determine if new refrigerator doors were airtight and adequately sealed.

I was one of the youngest employees in the department, which consisted of an elite group of workers. We earned an above-average hourly wage of $1.62 per hour. My father was a foreman at Kelvinator in a different department from where I worked, so we traveled to and from work together.

I did not own an automobile, nor did I intend to buy one, inasmuch as war was imminent, and I expected to become involved. I was dating a beautiful young lady who had been a classmate of mine at Catholic Central High School in Grand Rapids, Michigan.

At this time, gasoline was sixteen cents a gallon; premium oil was fifteen cents a quart; the finest theater in the city sold admission tickets for forty cents; and attending a "big band" dance held in the city's largest auditorium would cost about $2.50, including a corsage for my date.

Europe was already inflamed by what turned out to be World War II. Franklin D. Roosevelt was President, and although my mother was afflicted with a smoldering terminal abdominal cancer, our family and the country was apprehensive yet quite enthusiastic regarding our future.

My older sister, Margaret, and younger sister, Marianne, filled in for Mother on her bad days. Brother Bob, several years my junior, was engulfed with his schoolwork at Saint Joseph's School and was monitoring the progress being

One Soldier's Journey

made by the German Wehrmacht, their Storm Troopers, their SS Corps[1] and Panzer Divisions on both the Polish and Russian fronts.

These were complacent yet concerned times in our conservative city of Grand Rapids, Michigan. This, of course, had all changed after Japan's sneak attack on Pearl Harbor early Sunday morning, December 7, 1941, and when Congress declared war on Japan the following Monday, December 8. On December 11, 1941, Hitler and Mussolini, in separate speeches, declared war on the U.S. Now we were at war in Europe and in the Pacific. Thus, we were all made aware of the ominous events that would quickly engulf our entire nation in an unprecedented series of crises that would only be resolved by a total dedication to the war effort.

Rationing was promptly established to conserve our natural and manufactured resources of oil, gasoline, rubber (especially automobile tires) and various metals. Foods such as coffee, butter, cooking oils, sugar and meat were only a few examples of items that could only be purchased with allotted ration stamps dispensed by a neighborhood Ration Board[1]. We even had collection points for empty toothpaste tubes, which were made out of lead at that time. Aluminum pots and pans were collected. The aluminum was used to make airplanes, how being built in record numbers. Even bacon drippings were collected in the schools. We were told that these would be used in making bombs. Most of the meat, cheese, butter and chocolate candy went to the troops.

Automobile, appliance and heavy materials manufacturing plants were rapidly converted to the production of war machinery and materials consisting of ships, combat aircraft, tanks, artillery shells and guns, and small arms with their appropriate ammunition. Industry throughout the country was converted into a complete war arsenal devoted to defeating the enemy in order to preserve the freedom of the United States and our Allies. Young men were being drafted for duty in one of our military services.

These were the conditions of the country when my low draft lottery number of 188 was selected for early draft induction. On January 30, 1942, having passed all of my medical examinations, I officially became a bewildered

---

[1] The "SS" were Shutzstaffel, Hitler's elite troops; panzers were tanks.
[2] This was a national program, locally executed.

One Soldier's Journey

member of the United States Army. "Yes, Sir, Private Thome reporting, ready for action!"

Chapter 2

If It Fits

Camp Custer – Battle Creek, Michigan
February 1942

On that dark and early January morning, I had been ordered to report in downtown Grand Rapids on the sidewalk in front of the Grand Rapids Chamber of Commerce Building on Pearl Street. Here, along with a group of approximately thirty-five recently drafted young men, I anxiously waited for the arrival of the bus that would transport us to the area Induction Center located fifty miles south of Grand Rapids. This turned out to be Camp Custer Induction Center that was close to Battle Creek, Michigan. Emotions among these young men were extremely visible, especially as they hugged and kissed their mothers, sisters, girlfriends and wives goodbye, and as they also shook hands with their dads, little brothers and friends. When our bus arrived, we all boarded amid the cries of "Don't forget to write," "Don't volunteer for anything," and "Send us your new address as soon as possible." As black smoky exhaust spewed from the tailpipe of our bus, it roared to life and began to rumble south to the most incredible experience I could have ever imagined or predicted.

The bus trip to Camp Custer was noticeably quiet, and as daylight finally brightened the morning, most of the young occupants appeared deep in thought, staring out over the snow-covered Michigan countryside and perhaps contemplating their frightening futures.

Upon our arrival at the Induction Center, Camp Custer turned out to be a snarling beehive of hectic activity with the shouting of orders and the many directives vocalized in strange GI lingo. Paperwork, IQ testing, immunizations and the distribution of uniforms and equipment all came in rapid order. (During my military service, I received a total of 19 shots for various diseases – 3 Smallpox vaccinations, 5 Triple Typhoid, 4 Typhus shots, 6 Tetanus Toxoid and 1 Yellow Fever vaccine shot. Twenty years later, I still had Yellow Fever antibodies in my system.) Of course, unbeknown to us at the time, we were being prepared for our next adventure. That would be the start of an eight-week training cycle that the Army hoped would result in a proud and polished group of professional fighting men.

That first evening after a welcoming reception, a non-commissioned officer described the location of the mess hall, pay telephone booth and the PX (Post Exchange) where we could buy stamps for letters home. We were then led to a large two-story military barracks that housed approximately 60 men, 30 on each floor with appropriate toilets and showers in the near vicinity. Then, as darkness descended and taps was sounded across the post parade grounds signaling "lights out," a strange sickness, which was contagious and infectious, identified by muffled sighs and sobs, swept throughout our barracks. This sickness was diagnosed as "home."

One of my first experiences at Camp Custer was watching the revolting sight of sixty to seventy naked men standing in line, taking turns to bend over to "spread their cheeks." A non-com from the Medical Corps sat on a stool with a flashlight looking for hemorrhoids and then on to pubic hair looking for body lice. I questioned his decision to wear a mustache for what I thought was a high-risk assignment!

It was there where I learned how to "skin it back and milk it down." Also, it was there where I had my first "shit on a shingle" or "S.O.S." for breakfast composed of creamed chipped beef on a slice of toast. Of course, any meat that the menu claimed to be lamb or mutton was identified as goat meat.

When I was given size 11D shoes for my size 12AA feet, I was told that if I had a complaint I should get a "tough shit ticket" and have it punched by the Regimental Chaplain. When I received ten punches, I could obtain a three-day leave from camp. I believe that I actually inquired where I might be able to obtain one of those tickets!

After three days, the horrors of induction now seemed to be about over, and we were alerted that a troop train was being prepared on a nearby

One Soldier's Journey

sidetrack. We would learn that it would take us, along with another 300-400 new recruits, to a secret basic training center in an area of swamps, coral snakes and alligators. Four days later, dragging our equipment and army baggage, in absolute secrecy, we boarded a troop train that, we determined, was to head south from Michigan, and, hopefully, to a warm and sunny climate.

Chapter 3

Secret Passage

Camp Joseph T. Robinson – Little Rock, Arkansas
February 1942 – October 1942

    The strict enforcement of military secrecy upon our departure from the Camp Custer Induction Center made us all feel as if German black-shirted storm troopers were behind every shrub and bush and were mapping out our every move. Security, as I remember it, was most comical. We were instructed not to mention one word regarding our suspected destination either by phone or letter communication. This was considered so serious that we thought if the Germans got wind of our intentions, they would be over here raping our wives and girlfriends and enslaving our mothers in no time. The guilty GI culprits, we surmised, would soon be rotting in Leavenworth Military Prison listening to the sound of hammers building a scaffold.

    We all began to feel quite important and smug to think that the rise or fall of Nazi Germany rested on our shoulders. Consequently, I detected that we all stood a little straighter and taller during the frequent roll calls. Finally, reality set in and among the whistles, shouts and profanities of the non-coms (non-commissioned officers) from the permanent Camp Custer establishment, we were marched to a railroad siding and there waiting was a troop train consisting of approximately fifteen cars. Behold this rag tag collection of pathetic rookie soldiers, all out of step and cadence, dragging their government issue (GI) equipment, being loaded car by car, managed by some important-looking sergeant following orders printed on a clipboard.

One Soldier's Journey

The troop train left Battle Creek, Michigan, and Camp Custer late on a Thursday afternoon and roared south. Among the putrid odor of hot, sweaty bodies, stale cigarette smoke in cramped passenger cars, GI box lunches began to pop open and each soldier began to serve himself as his own personal chef. As darkness began to settle in, the windows of the train were covered so as not to reveal the whereabouts of this U.S. military machine of fighting soldiers to those sneaky German observation planes. Then, each soldier began to hunker down in his own little space in order to catch a fitful nap. We had no idea of our destination. We only knew that we were heading south.

Switching stops were made along the way with the usual jarring and bumping. After the "right of way" was established for those snorting and belching engines, we were again on our way. We were aware that we were still in civilized country because as our train slowed up, the warning, "ding, ding, ding," would let us know that, yes, we were now passing through some small rural town on our way to nowhere.

Finally, after a day and a half, window coverings were removed and our train appeared to slow down. After creeping along for an hour and a half of seemingly doubtful decisions, we stopped. We were then told that we had reached our destination and to immediately collect our gear and equipment and prepare to detrain.

As we stumbled out of our cramped quarters, non-commissioned officers were waiting for us. In groups of 150, we were ushered to temporary barracks for more roll calls, orientations, and above all, we were told that we were now stationed at Camp Joseph T. Robinson, Arkansas, which was situated in close proximity to Little Rock. We were also told that this would be our home for at least the next eight weeks. It was here where we would receive our basic training that would turn us into seasoned, professional, hardened soldiers completely ready for any combat mission.

It would be here that we would learn how to use the bayonet, the Browning automatic rifle, both the 60 and 81MM mortars, the Springfield, Enfield, and later, the Garand rifles. We would learn about machine guns, both the light and heavy, and how to disassemble and reassemble them under combat conditions. We would be taught how to use the bazooka, blow up bridges, use grenades both rifle and hand thrown, to identify poison gas and to use our gas mask for protection. "You, gentlemen, will be given hours and hours of physical exercise and close order drill and then when you are exhausted, a five-mile hike will be scheduled to end your day." This, of course, would all be extremely important in order to get us in physical condition needed to destroy the Germans.

Our first day at Camp Robinson, new soldiers were assigned various duties such as table waiting, KP duty, guard duty, etc. Directions to the mess hall, latrines (toilets), and showers were provided. The most important duty handed out was called "policing the area." This amounted to picking up cigarette butts and anything else, especially if it moved. To have a cigarette butt discovered in one's barracks area was equivalent to a high crime of treason.

All of these directives, plus a multitude of housekeeping chores, hanging up our clothes and arranging our underwear in our foot lockers according to the GI system, were our daily responsibilities. All the while, we were trying to remember and memorize our GI identification number as shown on our dog tags and the serial numbers on our rifles.

Chapter 4

This is the Army

Camp Joseph T. Robinson – Little Rock, Arkansas
February 1942 – October 1942

On the second day at my new station at Camp Joseph T. Robinson, the First Sergeant appeared in front of our morning formation, prior to our class of physical exercises, and called the roll of 200 inductees. He inquired if anyone in the formation could operate a typewriter, inasmuch as a company clerk was needed to type up duty rosters for KP, guard duty, charge of quarters, etc. The First Sergeant was standing right in front of me, so I quickly raised my hand, and at that moment I became "Company Clerk." As you can imagine, my name never appeared on any duty roster. Guess why!

At the end of Basic Training, all things changed, but with the job I now had, I really called the shots and avoided any and all of the Army's undesirable duties. However, there were certain jobs that had to be completed and certified, and then so noted in your Service Record. These consisted of rifle marksmanship bayonet training, gas warfare training and physical hygiene classes, in all of which I qualified.

At Camp Robinson, and at all other subsequent Army posts to which I was assigned, barracks life was a constant redundancy of letter writing, shoe shining, brass polishing, housekeeping (whether barracks or canvas huts) and equipment cleaning, not only among the newly inducted, but also among the hard-bitten veteran career soldiers.

One Soldier's Journey

Your rifle was your most respected piece of equipment. Its importance, as described by the Army, was such that you lived, breathed and slept with your rifle. The "sleeping with" was slightly exaggerated, but you needed to always remember that the wrath of God would descend upon you if you ever would fail to remember your rifle's serial number. I witnessed many instances when a soldier's weekend pass was revoked by some First Sergeant because the soldier failed to remember his rifle's serial number when quizzed.

Many tricks of property maintenance were quickly learned. For example, if by chance a drop or two of rifle-lubricating oil was spilled on the wooden barracks' floor, it was covered immediately by a puddle of lighter fluid and set ablaze. Like magic, the oil and lighter fluid would disappear without a trace or even a wood burn on the floor. This would have to be done immediately so that some "housekeeping" crazy non-com wouldn't see it. Brass polish was obtainable at the PX. Of course, the Army rule was, "if it's brass, it should shine." Kiwi and Shinola competed for shoe polish and one of those products, along with the right amount of spit, made "spit and polish" a reality. Upon induction, each soldier was issued two pairs of shoes. One pair was always kept under your bed to be displayed, highly shined and ready for inspection.

Finances were always a big concern, and the $21.00 a month salary was a real challenge. After deductions for Government Insurance, War Bonds, laundry and dry cleaning, there wasn't too much money left for the necessities required to survive. Cigarettes at the PX were only ten cents a package and admission to the post theater was only twenty-five cents. That helped, but it was always interesting to witness the exchange of money on payday. This was the day the big spenders were taken to task by the small spenders to return the borrowed money they had loaned them during the past month. Consequently, there was a constant exchange of money, back and forth, especially if one scored big in a crap game held under the blankets after "lights out."

Personal hygiene was quite an issue among the barracks dwellers. Cots were arranged in a head to toe configuration. If you wished to talk to your bedside buddy, you had to talk to his feet and he to yours. This arrangement was deemed necessary to avoid the head to head coughing and sneezing by your neighbor, which could cause air borne bacteria to be transmitted from one soldier to the next. As a result of such a practice, I did not experience the consequences of any large-scale epidemics from contagious flu or other respiratory illnesses.

The lack of regular bathing could result in a serious infraction of an unwritten law. Daily or evening showers were the norm, especially after long periods of physical activity as experienced during the rigors of basic training. The treatment given to a persistently unbathed soldier was the time honored "GI" scrub or bath. This consisted of a group of his barracks buddies taking the nude soldier into a shower and with a stiff GI scrub brush and a one pound bar of GI yellow laundry soap, giving a body scrub that bordered on torture. Because of that constant threat, we had the sweetest smelling soldiers in the entire Army.

When the eight weeks of Basic Training ended, a new group of trainees would arrive and the previous group would be transferred out and given assignments for specialized advanced training as MPs, Quartermasters, Engineers, Artillery, Medics, etc. I was "approached" about my advanced station and training. This was unheard of because one never knew in advance where his or her next assignment would be. I told First Sergeant Stanton Darling that I would like to remain at Camp Robinson. He promptly picked up the telephone, called the Post Headquarters and found me an assignment as clerk typist at the Post Personnel Office, Payroll Section.

In my new job at the Post Personnel Office, I typed up payroll rosters of our 800-man battalion each month, made out allotment requests, calculated payroll deductions for War Bonds and noted any deductions for court-martial fines that might be levied against a soldier's salary. Due to understaffing in the Post Personnel Office, this turned out to be a twelve-hour day job with every other weekend off.

Nevertheless, I was ecstatic because I was now engaged to be married to Marian A. Herrmann, the beautiful classmate of mine from Catholic Central High School, and I was now a corporal earning $36.00 a month instead of a private's pay of $21.00 per month. (Before I left for the Army, my mother gave me her diamond ring, which I had made into an engagement ring. I gave it to Marian on Christmas Eve, 1941, just before I was inducted the following January.) I quickly realized, though, that this rate of pay would be totally inadequate for a married man, especially when it was impossible to realize what the future would bring.

Chapter 5

Corporal to Lieutenant

Camp Joseph T. Robinson – Little Rock, Arkansas
Late October 1942

Although my assignment at the Post Personnel Office was cushy, prestigious and responsible, the days were long, arduous and eventually became quite boring due to the repetitive routines of the job, month after month. Just about the time when I thought I couldn't muster up the incentive to face another lackluster day, the chief warrant officer from our section stopped by my desk and said, "Corporal Thome, you're kind of a big[3] guy to be sitting behind a typewriter. If you don't object, I would like to recommend you for Officer Candidate School (OCS), because I believe that you would make an excellent infantry officer."

I was extremely flattered by his attention, even though I was aware that our troops had already landed in North Africa and that an invasion force to cross the English Channel was being assembled to attack fortress Europe. I jumped at the opportunity, however, because if I graduated from OCS as a second lieutenant, my salary would then increase to $250.00 per month, plus there would be many additional benefits. Also, the prestige and privileges of even a second lieutenant were enormous, and my bride-to-be would be delighted to have a military wedding. I could also foresee tailored uniforms, officer's club privileges and other niceties that were not extended to enlisted soldiers.

---

[3] I was 6 foot, 2 inches tall at the time.

One Soldier's Journey

I quickly agreed to participate in this new adventure. After the necessary transfer orders and paperwork were completed, I bid my Payroll buddies goodbye. George Bevington (Cleveland), Chuck Coddington (Detroit) and Joe Glickstien (New York) all shook my hand and bid me good luck, and "Jim, please write," while simultaneously admonishing me with, "You'll be sorry." This was late October of 1942, and it appeared now that a much anticipated Christmas furlough would be out of the question.

How prophetic was the advice I received? Nearly two years later, yes, I guess I was sorry. As I was lying in a shell hole outside of an apple orchard, among the hedgerows outside of Valognes de Puite in Normandy shortly after D-Day (June 6, 1944), I received my first mail from George Bevington back at Payroll. In his letter he stated, "Thome, things are so chicken shit back here, you can't believe it. You were lucky to get out when you did."

I thought at that time, my God, what would I give to trade my job with his. To be able to get every other Sunday off, see first-run movies at the Post Theater and enjoy a beer or two at the nearby PX would be a complete luxury. Even a smelly bus trip back and forth to Little Rock would be quite an improvement over the hedgerows and land mines in Normandy.

Prior to being accepted for my new assignment at Fort Benning and Officer's Training School, I had to go before a board of six examining officers at Camp Robinson for oral interrogation to determine if I was qualified to become an officer candidate. When I appeared before this board of officers, I was surprised to find that the board consisted of the Finance Officers of my Battalion. These were the same officers that I had been delivering typed payroll rosters to and with whom I had been doing other business for the past several months.

When I saluted and presented myself to them for questioning, I never received so much criticism and so many insults in my life. In front of me, they all agreed that I could never make it through officer training. In fact, they told me that I would probably embarrass the fine traditions of the U.S. Army. I left this meeting completely dejected and disappointed at my failure to qualify.

Three days later, my final appraisal appeared and I discovered that I had received an "excellent" rating from each officer on the inquiry board with the notation that I was highly qualified and that I would be a credit to the Officer Corps of the U.S. Army. This undoubtedly had been a pre-planned scam to worry me and perhaps was their idea of a practical joke to humble an ambitious corporal. Later, each one of these fine officers went out of his way to apologize for his behavior. I smiled and told them that I knew what they were doing to me, but I really didn't. So, off to Fort Benning, Georgia, and Officer's Candidate School to become a Second Lieutenant in the U.S. Army. My God, if I had only known what was to come!

Chapter 6

Nightmare of OCS

Fort Benning – Columbus, Georgia
November 1942 – January 1943

After arriving at Fort Benning's Officer's Candidate School in early November of 1942, I discovered OCS to be a regimented nightmare and a systematized process that made each candidate into a programmed clone of all the others. In ninety days ("ninety-day-wonders"), each one of us would be turned out as a graduated second lieutenant or else you would be busted out, a failure.

OCS was organized so that each candidate would rotate through various squad, platoon and company assignments, such as squad leader, platoon sergeant or acting platoon officer. At those times, you would have to demonstrate your ability to conduct close-order drills and other commands to display your leadership abilities. At the conclusion of these exercises, we would march out of our company area and report to classes in mortar, rifle marksmanship, and Browning automatic rifle, plus we had to be able to break down and know the nomenclature of each part of each of our weapons. All of this, plus classes in map reading, scouting and patrolling, hand-to-hand combat, demolitions, and defense and attack problem solving kept us busy late into every night.

After our evening meal, we would usually have inspection in our barracks with our disassembled rifles laid on a white towel on our wrinkle-free bed. Our clothing would have to be all in order, clean, all buttons intact, and may God help you if a speck of dust was on your spare pair of shoes. After inspection and during a little lull, you tried to study for your next graded examination given on any one of the subjects taught in class. All this time, First Lieutenant Leslie C. Hunter, our tactical officer, would silently observe our every move and record every little infraction. He would later confront those of us who he felt had horribly disregarded any of the sacred army traditions and regulations. Periodically, we would receive a private, personal review about these itemized infractions. One had better make sure that one could explain the reasons how such terrible disregard for army regulations and traditions could happen. You were then told how you were letting the U.S. Army down and because of that in no time German, Japanese and Italian soldiers would be over here ravishing our women and plundering our cities.

We started out with 30 men in my platoon, and each month we would have to grade one another. We would have to designate which candidate, in our opinion, would make the best officer, the second best and so on until the last man or thirtieth would be listed. Each candidate was given a numbered paper on which we ranked each man, from one to thirty, according to their ability to lead men and to perform the duties and exhibit the integrity of an officer. The slips of paper were then collected and compiled by our Company instructors, and generally the man or men who appeared consistently on the bottom of most the lists was "busted." This appraisal was performed several times during our 90-day course. The results were -- if you didn't like some candidate, you secretly placed him on the bottom 30 of your list.

Generally, as these grades were reported, the last man was usually dismissed as an officer candidate. Naturally, this turned out to be a popularity contest, and an unusual sweetness prevailed among the members of our training platoon, all hoping to land in the top quartile of our group.

Each morning, and before departure to the next training area for classes, Captain George R. Knauer, our company commander, would appear with a list of names that he would call out in alphabetical order. He would inform those men to fall out of ranks, return to their barracks and wait for further orders. The rest of us would then march out to our classes. Upon our return at the end of the day, those individuals who were called out earlier in the day, along with all their personal possessions, would be gone, their beds bare This was our first sign of a candidate being busted out of OCS. What a relief when Captain Knauer passed the T's and my name was not included on his "wash out" list. In retrospect, Officer's Training School became an experience where you were constantly either cursing the system or reflecting upon what an incredible experience it was in your life. It was much like playing football for Vince Lombardi or basketball for Bobby Knight. They were guys you hated, yet, you still felt proud and privileged to have played for them.

On December 10, 1942, shortly after I had entered OCS, my mother died following a long illness with cancer. She was 46 years old. The Red Cross and the Army cooperated in getting me home on leave to Michigan for the funeral. Arrangements were made for me to continue my training upon my return, although I would have to report to a different training company to catch up on the subjects I had missed while I was gone.

The Army was truly magnificent to me during this time. Post Headquarters dispatched an army sedan, usually reserved for staff and high-ranking officers, and chauffeured me back to my barracks from the machine gun range. At the barracks, I packed my clothes, signed the necessary paperwork and was transported to the Louisville & Nashville (L&N) Railroad Station with priority travel orders. I will never forget the sympathetic kindness expressed to me. I arrived home in time for the funeral.

Chapter 7

Graduation

Fort Benning – Columbus, Georgia
December 1943 – March 1, 1943

    In December, a Michigan winter is in stark contrast to that of Georgia. Yet, to be home during this Holiday Season was a joyful but saddened episode in my life. My older sister Margaret was now the matriarch of the family and she decided that a Christmas tree would be appropriate because, "That's what Mother would have wanted for the family."

    After Mother's funeral and after the holidays, I returned to Fort Benning and resumed my training. Now, however, I had to cope with the additional pressure of joining a new training company in order to catch up with what I had missed during my absence. The new company consisted of an entirely different group of guys with different personalities. I wondered how I could possibly compete as a perfect stranger on their popularity grading lists. Adding to the pressure was a newspaper clipping from the *Grand Rapids Herald*. It showed a picture of my fiancée with the following caption, "Betrothed announces her engagement and pending marriage to Officer Candidate James L. Thome, who will graduate as a second lieutenant in early March from the Infantry School, Fort Benning, Georgia."

    Of course, at this time, Marian had no idea that Captain Knauer, our Company Commander, was continuing his alphabetical "wash-out" list every morning and I still could be included on it. When I received this newspaper announcement, I immediately, in my mind, started to check out any ships listing

One Soldier's Journey

sailing dates to China. If I "washed out" now, I thought, my self-respect would be shattered and I would the first man aboard hoping that the trip would be real slow. Sadly, my bride-to-be would be abandoned, but my selfish, fragile ego would be spared.

Late in February 1943, it now appeared that graduation was at hand. Clothing salesmen and tailors appeared at the Fort from Columbus and started taking orders and measurements for officer uniforms. The government allowed each graduating officer a $250.00 allowance to purchase uniforms and the vendors from Columbus were most anxious to participate. They were aware that on graduation day we all had to be in our appropriate (new) military uniforms.

Just a few days before graduation, Captain Knauer appeared with his final "wash out" list. The two remaining Negro candidates in our company were busted. These two, in my opinion, were excellent career soldiers, were college graduates, were highly skilled in military knowledge and would have made excellent officers. These two were the last of the original nine Negro candidates of the group. Most of the men in my platoon were from the South as were the Tactical Grading Officers in the company, including Captain Knauer. I often wondered if these nine excellent Negro candidates were rated in the platoon's qualification, i.e., popularity, list as undesirable because of their race. I am certain that they were.

On February 28, 1943, an order was signed by John G. Handy, Lieutenant Colonel, Third Student Regiment, which Honorably Discharged me as Corporal, U.S. Army. On March 1, 1943, Thornton Chase, Colonel, Adjutant General Department, appointed me a Second Lieutenant, Infantry, in the Army of the United States.

I couldn't believe that I had survived this hellish but gratifying experience. When I entered Officer Candidate School, I was among 227 candidates in our training company, and now I was one of the 121 survivors who would graduate. From corporal, typist in the Payroll Section at Camp Joseph T. Robinson, to second lieutenant in ninety days - it was no accident that we were called "ninety-day-wonders." I accomplished in ninety days what a cadet at West Point accomplishes in four years. It was truly heady stuff. (Well, I have to admit that we probably had a stripped-down modified version of the four-year program.)

My next project was now my impending wedding. As I rode via the L&N Railroad to Chicago and then connected to Grand Rapids, I reflected on my future and just where destiny would take me. Troops were being assembled in

England for the impending invasion of Europe, and it was almost guaranteed that junior officers would be the first casualties of that invasion. I was now certain that I was expendable as a replacement and that it would be very possible that I might leave my young bride a widow. As you will see later, there were many occasions when this could have happened.

Chapter 8

A Wedding and First Assignment

Grand Rapids, Michigan to Fort McClellan, Anniston, Alabama
March 6, 1943 – May 1943

    At midnight on March 5, 1943, it began to snow and by the morning of March 6 ten inches of heavy, white snow was covering the Michigan spruce, pine and hemlock trees. It was a beautiful, picturesque, pristine winter wonderland for my wedding day.

    At 10:00 AM[4], at the altar of St. Mary's Catholic Church on Turner Avenue in Grand Rapids, Michigan, I pledged my love, devotion and loyalty to my young, beautiful bride, whom I now felt that I hardly knew, before Reverend Bernard Hansknecht and small group of immediate family, relatives and friends. During the ceremony and while my vows were intoned and before my "I do" response, I reflected on my future. How could I possibly live up to the responsibilities and to the solemn commitment I was about to make? This was a confusing and bewildering time of war, and it seemed as if everyone was living in the present, not knowing what tomorrow might bring.

    After a short reception at the Cherie Inn on Lake Drive and Cherry Streets near downtown Grand Rapids, my bride and I left for the railroad station for our short train ride to Chicago to honor our reservations at the Hotel Sherman our first wedding night. When we arrived at the Hotel Sherman, the lights in their

---

[4] At times, I will use military time which is a 24-hour clock. For example, 0100 hours is 1:00 AM; 1000 hours is 10:00 AM, 2300 hours is 11:00 PM.

world famous College Inn were dimmed, as were all of the bistros in Chicago. We were at war and lights, spirits and futures were all dimmed.

Prior to my departure from OCS for my wedding, I had received my first assignment as an officer. My instructions were to report to Fort McClellan in Alabama. This was the location of an Infantry Replacement Training Center located near Anniston. I was assigned to be a platoon leader and, I, with the help of several non-commissioned officers, had the mission to teach a unit of forty raw recruits the science of modern warfare. These young Army inductees were all very homesick and I wanted desperately to alleviate their concerns and fears. Already, I was aware that my responsibilities were not only to these young men but also to their wives, sweethearts, parents, friends and relatives that were left at home. I was also aware that whatever I did to affect their lives would also be reflected in their letters back home. I wanted all that were left at home to know that Lieutenant Thome was really a good, understanding officer who was looking out for their sons and loved ones.

My bride and I had a few days leave before reporting to camp and we used that time apartment hunting. After a bit of searching, we finally found a room in a private home in Anniston and I commuted back and forth to Fort McClellan by bus. All of our meals were eaten "out" except when I was at camp. Reflecting back, I'm almost certain that my new bride was homesick in Anniston and wondered how she got caught up in this frantic whirlpool of army life.

During this time, German troops were massing on the French and Belgium borders and the winds of war were swirling across the European continent while the rumors of the Jewish Holocaust became more and more revealing. Our invasion of Europe was seeming more and more that it was going to become reality. Consequently, new combat infantry divisions were being quickly organized, one of which was the 63rd Infantry Division commanded by Brigadier General Louis E. Hibbs.

On May 21, 1943, Special Order #119, Headquarters, Fort McClellan, Alabama, directed my transfer to the 63rd Infantry Division located at Camp Blanding, Florida, located about forty miles southwest of Jacksonville. There, my mission was to train and condition new recruits for the coming invasion of Europe.

When I received these orders, my bride returned home to Grand Rapids while I proceeded to Camp Blanding. There, I reported to the commanding

One Soldier's Journey

general. The cadre personnel immediately prepared and made plans to receive and house our new recruits. We were to mold them into a fighting unit that would reflect considerable credit to our training program, our division, and to the United States fighting forces. We were all gung ho and our esprit-de-corps was unbounded.

Chapter 9

How It Was

Fort McClellan – Anniston, Alabama
March 1943 – May 1943

    It was interesting for me to observe that the transitional period from a peacetime army to a wartime footing was met with somewhat bitter and profound resistance, especially among the career enlisted men and among the officer corps. It was true that during this period many officers who were captains and majors during peacetime suddenly found themselves promoted to lieutenant colonels and colonels found themselves promoted to brigadier generals due to the rapid expansion of the Army. For them, it seemed very difficult to cancel all those peacetime Saturday night formal dances at the Officers' Clubs in order to make it appear that an all-out war effort was being made. This observation was especially true while I was stationed at an army "fort," which was very different than an army "camp."

    Fort Benning, Georgia, and Fort McClellan, Alabama, were "forts" classified as permanent army posts with barracks usually made of brick for the top grade enlisted non-coms. Officers' quarters were usually single family, permanent homes. Of course, the usual pecking order prevailed, and housing was assigned according to rank. The fort commanding general, usually a career officer, had the biggest home available. It was maintained both inside and out by enlisted personnel. Junior officers, consisting of lieutenants and some senior non-commissioned officers, usually found themselves in quarters best described as upscale chicken coops, although they too were single one-family homes.

One Soldier's Journey

On the other hand, an army "camp" was a temporary wartime emergency training establishment adequately equipped with the necessary amenities such as a Post Exchange, Post Theater and recreational equipment for gymnastics and other physical training activities. The barracks were wooden, heated by coal-burning stoves. In many instances, our enlisted personnel were quartered in tent-like structures covered by canvas with wooden floors. Officers were quartered in wooden barracks much like those assigned to enlisted men stationed at an Army fort. At both installations, officers and enlisted men had separate mess halls, latrines/showers, and social activities.

After World War II started and while US forces were landing and dying in North Africa, the tempo of training and preparing trained replacement soldiers increased dramatically. Leisure time was almost non-existent, yet on weekends, in order to maintain morale, passes to nearby towns were made available to selected soldiers on a quota basis. An excellent way to maintain discipline and prevent bad behavior was to threaten to deny a weekend pass.

Boomtowns, as they were called, sprang up outside of every army base camp. Usually many of the boomtown young ladies would station themselves outside of the main camp gates in order to meet, entertain and perhaps to bring home some soldier for dinner. This being the case, before leaving camp every departing soldier had to produce a condom to prove that he had VD protection as encouraged by the Medical Corps.

Also, in each major community in close proximity to an army base, the Medical Corps would establish Prophylactic Stations manned by Medical Corps personnel. These stations were set up to treat soldiers who might have had a sexual encounter, did not use a condom and were suspicious that their partners might be infected. This program was very strict and, consequently, there were no excuses if a soldier became infected. In fact, if a soldier did become infected through neglect and became hospitalized or confined to quarters, pay for that period was deducted for the duration of the illness. I might add that during those years there was no quick cure for sexually transmitted diseases since penicillin type drugs were not yet available.

Chapter 10

On the Move

Camp Blanding – Jacksonville, Florida
May 21, 1943 – August 1943

    At Camp Blanding, Florida while we were fighting the sand fleas, chiggers, coral snakes and alligators, we all imagined that we could make the fighting 63rd Division the liberating force in Europe. Thus, during our practice field maneuvers, we all pretended that behind every palmetto, cypress or slash pine tree lurked a fanatic Nazi waiting to ambush us.

    There was a considerable delay in receiving our filler recruits in order to bring our new division up to full strength. During this lapse, we officers and the cadre of non-commissioned officers busied ourselves cleaning, painting and generally renovating an abandoned and dilapidated army camp in order to make these quarters brighter and more comfortable for our new inductees. Also, in order to hone our skills, we reviewed the infantry subjects we were to teach. In so doing, considerable days were spent on the ranges firing our light and heavy machine guns, bazookas, rifles, carbines and mortars. Even the artillery personnel identified an acceptable impact area where they could practice shooting their 105mm and 155mm artillery pieces at imaginary German Tiger tanks.

    North at Jacksonville, the city was teeming with navy and army personnel since military installations were in the nearby vicinity. Despite the overcrowding of this area, my new wife Marian returned from Michigan. Together we found a rare, but desirable, one-room apartment in a home that also housed our "across

One Soldier's Journey

the hall" neighbors, Bob and Peg Otis. They were from Fulton, New York, and were also recently married and caught up in the service. Bob belonged to our Division Military Police Unit. The four of us formed a very warm and cordial friendship, especially Marian and Peggy. They kept each other company while Bob and I were at camp during the week. Each weekend, Bob and I would take the bus back and forth between Jacksonville and camp. In order to avoid the long lines waiting to board the buses, Bob would wear his Military Police (MP) armband and take my arm and escort me to the front of the line. I am certain that to many of the soldiers waiting, it appeared that Bob had arrested an army lieutenant and was escorting him back to camp. Bob survived the war and eventually became Chief of Police in his hometown.

During this lull and before the new filler troops arrived, an almost peacetime atmosphere existed at Camp Blanding. Small social activities took up our time. The wives always seemed to have some type of social event planned such as dances at the Officers' Club, wedding receptions or bridge games. They also helped to decorate and furnish the day rooms at camp. Even though these social activities helped to create a diversion from our real mission, in our little group of soldier friends there was always the question of, "What's next?"

Early in August of 1943, we received a directive from the Fifth Army Headquarters, Atlanta, Georgia, that changed our designated mission from jungle warfare to a European mission. We were thus directed to move to terrain more adaptable to that type of fighting. We were also told that in order to implement this new order, we had to move our entire division of men, trucks, vehicles, medical equipment, army materiel and personnel by way of a motor convoy. From Camp Blanding near Jacksonville, we were to convoy across the panhandle of Florida, through Alabama, into Mississippi, to our new location at Camp Van Dorn, which was located about thirty miles west of McComb, Mississippi.

Upon receipt of these new orders, many of the wives quickly departed by train and bus to be first to locate apartments off base in order to be with their husbands. Our motorized convoy followed across Alabama, bivouacking among the cotton, corn and even some tobacco fields along the way. This was a sharp contrast to the frosty rigors of a Michigan autumn.

Chapter 11

Here They Come!

Camp Van Dorn – McComb, Mississippi
September 23, 1943 – April 19, 1944

We finally arrived at our abandoned, yet partially rehabilitated, encampment. The idyllic serenity of the countryside was striking. Was this the calm before the arrival of 6,000 recruits that would be necessary to make our new 63rd Division a viable fighting force? At this time, we still had a skeleton crew of training cadre, the same crew we had at Camp Blanding. Again, we had a multitude of housekeeping chores to complete, the same as at our previous camp, in order to make the new quarters inviting and comfortable for our new recruits. The scrubbing, repairing and painting was endless. In the evening at twilight as darkness set in, we could sometimes hear the harmonizing of Maxine, LaVerne and Patti Andrews from some far off PX jukebox. Then, the sound of taps would echo across the distant parade grounds announcing "good night" to a bunch of bone-tired and exhausted soldiers who were mostly thinking of home.

The storm broke about ten days after our arrival at our new camp. In late September 1943, at the caMPs railhead, newly-inducted recruits began to emerge from railroad cars, spilling out like an overcooked pot of rice. The troop train was discharging young men in an endless stream that our reception committee peeled off as they emerged and instantly formed them into platoons, companies and battalions. They were then marched off to their respective barracks areas, and in so doing, their induction into the 63rd Infantry Division was complete.

One Soldier's Journey

I remained assigned to Company C, 253rd Infantry Regiment as executive officer. Lieutenant Hubert M. Nance, Commanding, and Lieutenants Marty Herpolshiemer, Paul Prickett, Greg Sandker and Pete Troglio as platoon leaders staffing the remaining assignments. Discipline was immediately established with our very competent non-commissioned personnel, and the intense training of infantry skills also began immediately.

On October 6, 1943, I received a very complimentary letter for my troop de-training efforts from Headquarters, 253rd Infantry Regiment, Camp Van Dorn, Mississippi, signed by Lieutenant Colonel Marion W. Schewe. It reads:

Dear Lieutenant Thome;
I want to personally thank you and your hutment guides for the splendid job that you as a team accomplished in handling the filler groups for this Regiment.
Your attention to duty, and the speed and thoroughness with which you handled your men won the admiration of the Regiment. You received the highest comments from the Commanding General and his staff.
Thank you.
s/Marion W. Schewe, Lt. Col., Inf., Commanding

On October 25, 1943, my company's leading and teaching activities were interrupted when I was admitted to the Camp Van Dorn base hospital with an infection in my right foot and leg. This was an interruption that I strongly resisted because of my desire to remain with my company.

Marian visited me several times during my ten-day stay in the hospital in spite of the difficulties of traveling to and from the hospital by bus from our apartment in McComb, a distance of forty miles. Consequently, my discharge from the hospital came as a great relief to both of us. Our apartment in McComb was in a private home also occupied by Lieutenant Ted Sosney and his wife who were a delightful couple and great friends. Lieutenant Sosney was an attorney from Milwaukee in private life before the war.

The process of training new recruits continued. We finally progressed from basic training to continued advanced training in attack and defense maneuvers. This occupied many busy days as we prepared our division for combat. Then, on January 8, 1944, Special Order #6, Headquarters 63rd Division, signed by First Lieutenant Clement J. Coss, directed me to report for special duty. I was ordered to train an elite group of volunteer soldiers to participate in the 63rd Division Ranger School and thus to prepare this group to be the main assault effort of our division on the coast of France.

The group consisted of extremely brave, heroic and dedicated patriotic Americans who were determined to defeat Hitler and the Japanese. Training consisted of the usual infantry subjects but fine-tuned to a much higher level of expertise. Exhaustive physical training, hand-to-hand fighting, bayonet training, and, again, rifle marksmanship were the subjects most emphasized. This amounted to a four-week course.

On graduation day, I led our new rangers on an eight hour, twenty-five mile, forced march with each man carrying a full field pack and rifle. Thus, at the end of each four-week ranger cycle, I had this honor. For me, this graduation exercise was an exhaustive, demanding duty, which, unknown to me at this time, really prepared me physically for my landing on Utah Beach six months later.

For my efforts with the 63rd Division Ranger School, I was promoted to First Lieutenant, effective January 18, 1944, War Department Special Order #5, by direction of the President.

(As of this writing, Lieutenant Prickett died in 1999, Lieutenant Sandker died in 1974, Lieutenant Troglio died in 1980, Lieutenant Coss died in 1994, Lieutenant Hubert M. Nance died in 1975, and Colonel Schewe died in 1992. Lieutenant Sosney, Captain Savoia and Lieutenant Herpolsheimer have not been located, and it is not known whether or not they are still alive.)

Chapter 12

Off to War

Camp Van Dorn – McComb, Mississippi
April 18, 1944

Looking back to that warm September day of 1943, while I was standing by the arriving troop trains filled with young soldier inductees, I was bitterly disappointed by not seeing any young Japanese-Americans detraining among the assemblage of young men. I had become acquainted with some of these extremely patriotic and dedicated young Americans while at Camp Robinson. Most were volunteers and most were inducted from the west coast while their families and relatives were rounded up and placed in isolated concentration camps somewhere in the United States due to their suspected and presumed threat to our national security. This was a sordid and despicable episode in U.S. history as displayed by its reaction toward anyone who was of Japanese heritage.

While at Camp Robinson, I had discovered that these young Japanese Americans were absolutely devoted to the United States and were most eager to prove their uncompromising patriotism. They were fastidious in their personal habits and discipline while their performance in response to direction and instruction was absolutely impeccable. Even though my platoon at Camp Van Dorn was being filled with inductees from all geographical areas of our country, wonderful young men from many different races and backgrounds, I remained very disappointed that I did not have the privilege of having a few of the Japanese-Americans under my command. At Camp Robinson, they were forever smiling and never complained.

I later learned that these young men who had been trained at Camp Robinson were later transferred to the 442nd Japanese-American Infantry Battalion. They fought the Germans in the Italian mountain country and became known as the "Purple Heart Battalion." Their casualties were enormous, as was their heroism. They experienced no fewer then 8,500-battle casualties. They received more medals for bravery than any other fighting unit in the U.S. Army. Nineteen received the Medal of Honor. While all this was going on, their loved ones remained in concentration camps, places like the one at the Minidoka Relocation Center in Idaho. Incarcerating these innocent and loyal citizens was one of the poorest decisions ever made by our U. S. government.

When I was relieved from Special Duty at the Division Ranger School, I returned to my platoon and company activities and was promptly assigned to become our company's mess officer. My duties were to oversee the operation of the kitchen, the meal menus and services. As mess officer, I discovered that I soon became the recipient of many unusual and unwritten entitlements. The mess sergeant would extend to me many special favors in order to avoid a reprimand for deviating from the daily army recommended menu and/or how meals were prepared and served. Because of my understanding and perhaps due to my leniency toward the system, I would frequently find a cherry pie or chocolate cake mysteriously appear on the desk in my quarters. I never questioned this miracle or wondered how this could happen, but occasionally I would receive a very sly and shielded wink from one of my very capable cooks.

Another very welcome highlight of my mess duty was when Lieutenant Bruno J. Savoia from Headquarters Company would receive a gallon tin of raw oysters from his parents who owned a cannery outside of New Orleans. This would result in an oyster feast down at the mess hall with a select group of his officer friends. My kitchen crew would be the first to supply us with adequate amounts of cocktail sauce and shrimp dip. Happy days under a threatening sky.

As the drums of war began beating louder, I was issued Special Order #97, Headquarters, Camp Van Dorn, Mississippi, dated April 18, 1944, that directed me and thirty three other second and first lieutenants to be processed as overseas replacements. This was our signal that the invasion of Europe was fast approaching, since that order was supplemented by another order, which directed a considerable number of reinforcements consisting of privates and privates first class to prepare for overseas duty as well.

I received medical clearance for overseas duty from John J. Redman, M.D., Captain, Medical Corps, on April 19, 1944. On that same day, I said good-bye to the warm Mississippi evenings, to my platoon, Company C, to the echo of bugle calls and mockingbirds in the distance and to my beloved 63rd Division.

One Soldier's Journey
"Good-bye to you all and may God bless and protect you until we all meet again in Berlin."

Chapter 13

Countdown to Battle

Fort George G. Mead – Baltimore, Maryland
April 19, 1944 – May 2, 1944

    My new transfer orders specified that, after a nine-day delay, I was to report to Fort Meade, a large, sprawling military establishment in Maryland, designated as a staging depot. It was there that overseas-designated soldiers were equipped with proper clothing and equipment for overseas duty in Europe.

    After receiving my transfer orders, I quickly gathered up my possessions at camp and, with Marian, began to proceed to Michigan by bus, train and taxi. After settling into a temporary apartment, in accordance with military advice, I reviewed my Last Will and Testament, Power of Attorney and made sure that all of my insurance documents were in order in preparation for the possibility that I might become a war casualty. The few remaining days home were spent at a summer cottage at Spring Lake, Michigan, a small resort community on the eastern shores of Lake Michigan.

    Those frantic last days were filled with panic, concerns and expectations, especially after Marian announced that she was pregnant with our first child. I was filled with awe upon the news of becoming a first-time father, yet at the same time felt terribly apprehensive about my overseas assignment since we both anticipated a prolonged separation at the time of the baby's birth.

    As the countdown continued toward my departure, I received many "good luck" handshakes and embraces from friends and relatives, plus their generous offers of prayers and novenas for my safe return. I welcomed every one.

One Soldier's Journey

The military furnished me with the necessary prepaid travel vouchers in order for me to arrive at Fort Meade within their mandated timetable. I chose instead to spend another day at home and elected to call the Operations Officer at Romulus Air Force Base in suburban Detroit in hopes of hitching a ride to Fort Meade. (Military officers, at that time, had the privilege of hitch hiking on an available military plane in order to reach their next transfer station.) I was informed that a B-24 bomber was departing the next afternoon for Westover Field, Massachusetts. I was told that if I reported to "Operations" at the Air Force Base on time, space would be available.

Early the next morning, I quickly packed and with my wife, my sisters, and my brother departed for the air base in our family automobile, driven by my father. Upon arrival at Romulus, I paid "Operations" a $2.00 deposit for a parachute. As the B-24 was warming up on the tarmac in preparation for takeoff, I said my good-byes and ran across the runway, my parachute bumping along beside me, and claimed my reserved seat.

Two hours later, after an uneventful flight, we landed at Westover where I surrendered my parachute and recovered my $2.00 deposit. The Air Force commander at the base graciously supplied me with a jeep and driver who transported me to the railroad station in Boston. After a very rapid trip along the East Coast, I arrived and reported at Headquarters, Fort Meade, Maryland. I had arrived one day early.

I could hardly believe the incredible progression of events that had transpired within the past few days. The shocking realization was suddenly beginning to set in that I was now on a very long and dangerous journey, destination unknown, and entirely beyond my control.

I remained at Fort Meade just long enough to be furnished with overseas clothing and equipment. Those items included a .30 caliber carbine, ammunition magazines, carbine cleaning equipment, canteen and a First Aid kit containing sulfa powder which was, at that time, considered a miracle drug, designed to save lives in case of a bullet wound or some other exposed injury. All of these remained with me until I landed on the coast of France.

Chapter 14

Out to Sea

Camp Myles Standish & Boston Harbor – Boston, Massachusetts
May 3, 1944 – May 12, 1944

On May 3, 1944, I was ordered to Camp Myles Standish, Massachusetts along with several other Infantry officers, who were designated as overseas replacements for combat casualties. Camp Myles Standish was the point of embarkation from the port of Boston.

The day after my arrival, I discovered that my name was posted on the bulletin board in the Officer's Quarters for special duty. I noted that for the next three days I was assigned to the post stockade as Provost Marshal. There, I was to replace the regular assigned officer who had received a three-day leave. I also discovered that a Provost Marshal was the equivalent to a prison warden, a position for which I was totally untrained.

About the time I relieved the permanent CO (commanding officer) at the stockade, there were approximately 400 prisoners incarcerated. Most of the prisoners were black and had been picked up by the Military Police for being AWOL and /or for desertion. They were all waiting for trial in the military courts. These young men were all convinced that in combat they would be sacrificed by being used as "night fighters", and they were desperate in their resolve to avoid that destiny by any and all means possible. They would do anything to prevent it.

The stockade covered approximately two acres and contained comfortable barracks quarters for the prisoners. The entire area was encircled by two barbed-

One Soldier's Journey

wire fences that were about six feet apart. Entry to the compound was made through two double gates. Machine guns on towers were manned at each corner and mid-way between each corner.

Twenty minutes after command responsibilities were exchanged and I accepted my new assignment, one of the MP sergeant guards rushed into my office. "One of the prisoners appears to be going berserk in the latrine!" he exclaimed. The latrine was located to the extreme rear of the stockade. Six of the Military Police on duty at that time decided that we should all enter the stockade together in order to determine the extent of the disturbance.

Quickly, we discovered a prisoner wielding a heavy, metal, mop handle. He was in the process of smashing wash basins, toilet bowls and anything else that was breakable. Four of the guards seized him and pinned him to the floor and were then able to get an arm lock on him. As we proceeded to remove him from the stockade, the prisoner broke loose and stood glaring wildly, eyes dilated, frothing at the mouth. At that particular moment, one of the guards, in a tower adjacent to us called down and shouted, "Stand back, Lieutenant! I'll shoot the nigger son-of-a-bitch."

At that instant, about 300 prisoners closed in around the MP guards and me. One of the prisoners stepped forward, poked his finger in my chest and informed me, "Lieutenant, if anything happens to our brother, they will never find a trace of you or these MPs again. You will be chopped up into little pieces and the earthworms will eat you; clean job; no trace."

Thinking quickly, I informed the threatening prisoner that our brother was sick and would he please help me to get him out of the stockade and into an ambulance for a quick trip to the base hospital. I then saw a miracle happen. He quickly called those three hundred prisoners to attention, formed them into a column of fours and marched them to the far end of the stockade. There he left them and returned. He saluted me and thanked me for my understanding of their helpless predicament. I have often wondered what might have happened in that stockade at Camp Myles Standish if my reaction to the situation had been different.

The final few days at camp were spent packing. We separated our "hold" baggage from our "carry on" baggage, mailed unneeded possessions back home, wrote good-bye letters to our loved ones and informed those back home of our new Army Post Office (APO) numbers in order to receive overseas mail. All this time we were listening closely to the progress of the war as reported from London by Edward R. Murrow.

We received our departure orders on May 12, 1944. As the two and one half-ton Army truck transported us to the docks in Boston Harbor that day, I observed a huge crowd of military service people teeming in the streets of Boston. Army, Navy, Airforce, Marines, WACS, SPARS and WAVES, plus other supportive branches of the various services were represented. All seemed deep in thought, and all appeared to be concentrating on their futures. Most of them were in Boston for only one purpose, to say goodbye to America.

We boarded our ship, the *USS General Meigs*, a transport Liberty ship that was one of a quickly-assembled convoy of 44 vessels of all kinds and descriptions. Most were troop carriers. However, according to the rumors, many contained tanks, planes and assorted motor vehicles. One of the most exciting rumors, especially among the young soldiers aboard our ship, was that one of those ships out there in our convoy contained more than 500 young, beautiful and passionate Army nurses. Thus, considerable time was spent as we crossed the wild Atlantic contemplating just which ship those nurses were on.

My quarters, a small stateroom that I shared along with another officer, were comfortable, clean and adequate compared to the large dormitory quarters in the hold section where the enlisted men were quartered. Meals were served in the Officers' Mess for the ship's officers. The enlisted men were served cafeteria style off from the main deck. The shipboard food was tasty and was served in an excellent manner by the ship's crew who all expressed concern for our future.

On the day we sailed, approximately two miles off the port of Boston, four Navy destroyers appeared to become our escorts. They took positions about a mile ahead of our convoy's lead ship. There they scurried back and forth like beagle hounds on the scent of a rabbit, all the while looking for Hitler's wolf pack of submarines. Several depth charges were detonated along the way but we never learned of any results from their explosions.

The North Atlantic in the month of May was horrendous. Always a concern were the giant waves, squalls and the never-ending threat of enemy torpedoes blowing us all into the depths of the icy waters. At one point, I became so nauseous that I would have welcomed the hit of an enemy torpedo.

Chapter 15

"Ten Shilling Hill"

Warminster Barracks – Whitchurch, England
Mid-May 1944 – Mid-June 1944

On May 18, 1944, after five and a half days of sailing in the perilous waters of the North Atlantic, we finally sighted the coast of Northern Ireland. As we entered the North Channel and passed by the Isle of Man, many of us aboard raised our eyes to heaven and thanked God. We were scheduled to dock immediately at Liverpool Harbor but due to the considerable maritime traffic, we were delayed for two days.

Finally, our ship was cleared to dock. As we were piloted and tugged dockside, we were greeted by a large number of young ladies all shouting, "Nylons?" These were the "Liverpool Lassies," all receptive, cordial and extremely amorous toward the American GI's. They were all hoping to receive scarce "goodies" from the States. As it turned out, these were the same young ladies who insisted that their new soldier boyfriends include a blanket on a date and who also insisted that pregnancy was impossible if intercourse was performed standing up. This was a paradox that I never did quite understand. Blankets? Standing up?

After we came ashore, lorries[5] whisked us away, along with our "hold" and personal baggage, to Casual Detachment, 222nd Replacement Company Camp #83, located about 50 kilometers south of Liverpool and approximately 15

---

[5] "Lorries" were the British equivalent of "trucks."

kilometers east of Chester, situated next to the Royal Tank Corps' encampment at Warminster Barracks. It was here where I experienced the "luxury" of a cold shower and a straw-filled mattress while trying to figure out the mystery of "ten shilling hill."[6]

On our journey from the docks of Liverpool, we passed through Chester and then arrived in the late afternoon at Whitchurch, which was near the Warminster Barracks. Units of the Royal Tank Corps at Warminster Barracks had already departed for the Channel ports in preparation for the coming invasion and our officer group inherited their vacated billets. These were two-story stone structures of old English architecture, six rooms to each building with six officers sharing each large room. Since there was no central heating, each room had its own fireplace. A large adjacent building served as a mess hall.

This time of the year, the English countryside was absolutely beautiful. Everything was a brilliant green, clean and orderly. It was a place of calm, peace and tranquillity. In contrast, within the large metropolitan areas of London, Birmingham, Bristol, Plymouth, Liverpool and Southampton, calls were going out to marshal all the little British children to safer locations in the country's rural areas. There they could avoid the incessant bombing by the Germans, which was causing death and injury to the innocents.

The morning after our arrival at Warminster Barracks, off in the misty distance, I observed a wooded park-like hill with an approximate 600-foot elevation, just beyond the caMPs parade grounds and the guarded gates of our complex. On the approach to this hill were double lines of soldiers who appeared to be waiting, not unlike a chow line by the kitchen or at the box office of an Oscar-winning film production. I soon discovered that this was the famous "ten shilling hill" that I had heard so much about. This was the hill where passionate young soldiers could relieve their sexual needs by visiting accommodating and patriotic young British ladies.

I inquired about this unbelievable phenomenon from one of the British staff officers at the barracks. His response was, "Hill, what hill?" A sympathetic psychologist might suggest that this was an amusing case of denial. I often wondered if someone received a commission from this activity. This was wartime, so who cared.

---

[6] A shilling was equal to 12 pence, or 1/20 of a British pound.

One Soldier's Journey

I later learned that each young lady, a credit to the crown, would work a six-hour shift and would relieve each one of the 36 soldiers she would accommodate during her shift of ten shillings. The "hill" operated around the clock and there was no lack of eager, young GI customers. I quickly calculated that each young lady would generate about $72.00 per shift, which at that time was an excellent salary, especially if one enjoyed one's work.

Three days after settling into our new home at Warminster Barracks, I was given command of a "replacement package" of 200 enlisted men and non-commissioned officers who would be used later as replacements for D-Day casualties. We had a continuous training program scheduled that consisted of night infiltration, demolitions, scouting, patrolling, hand-to-hand combat and other required infantry skills. Of course, we all knew that this training schedule was a deliberate means to avoid boredom while we waited for our turn to cross the English Channel.

Finally, at daybreak on June 6, 1944, while my company slowly returned to our barracks from an extended overnight exercise of infiltrating enemy lines, the sky erupted with literally thousands[7] of Allied aircraft heading toward the English Channel. All were painted with identifying stripes across their wings and fuselages. Instantly, we all knew that the waiting was over and our invasion of the Germans in Normandy was now at hand.

Back in the barracks, ears were glued to the BBC radio news reports of our Allied success, but they just didn't seem to come. Could it be that our invasion was a failure? A furious eruption of letter writing to loved ones back home took place and no one could concentrate on the usual evening poker games. We were all worried that our Allied forces would experience another Dieppe off the coast of France and that Hitler would once again drive us back into the sea.

---

[7] There were 822 aircraft carrying parachutists or towing gliders; 13,000 aircraft in the attack armada.

Chapter 16

Crossing the English Channel and Utah Beach

Utah Beach – Normandy, France
June 15, 1944

    On June 6, 1994, while my company of replacements were relaxing in our mess hall drinking coffee and resting from our midnight infiltrating exercise, unknown to us at the time, thousands of our Allied troops composed of American, British and Canadian soldiers were storming the fortified shores of France. This was the largest air/sea/land assault in the history of warfare. Although we were far removed from the action, we were able to hear the rumble of battleship cannons firing salvos in support of our troop landings. The well-documented heroic actions of our airborne support troops, fighter, glider and bomber pilots and their crews will be long remembered. That night, as darkness descended, dozens of searchlights lit up the skies, poking holes in the clouds searching for enemy aircraft.

    As the ebb and flow of battle continued on the beaches, Utah, Omaha, Sword, Juno, and Gold, most of the men remaining back in our quarters intensified their pursuit of excellence in infantry skills. All thoughts of "ten shilling hill" came to an abrupt halt. Many started to hone and sharpen their bayonets, clean and oil their rifles and check their battle equipment. Everyone was thinking when would it be our turn.

One Soldier's Journey

On June 14, 1944, Order #50, Headquarters 15 Replacement Depot, WBS SOS ETSOUSA, APO 67, directed that I was now relieved from my training company and would be transferred to the 11th Officer Replacement Depot, APO 131, Replacement Detachment X-24-B. I was now included in Shipment #16 D12163 which was my channel crossing shipping orders. Early the next morning of June 15, 1944, I, along with several officers from Warminster Barracks, was transported to Plymouth, a channel seaport and a port of departure to France.

Plymouth, by all appearances, was a frenzied conglomeration of troops from all branches of the service and of all nationalities milling about waiting for boarding orders, plus stacks and stacks of materials consisting of rations, medical supplies, jerry cans of gasoline and mountains and mountains of clothing. Transportation Corps personnel who wore color-coded armbands or replacement detachment numbers marshaled everyone to their respective assembly areas. Transportation officers with their ever-present clipboards charged back and forth shouting orders while directing troops and the flow of priority traffic to their proper ship assignments for the impending channel crossing.

Five other officers and I were assigned to a medium sized channel boat along with about 500 enlisted men that were quartered in a large hold section of the ship. The men all carried forty pound field packs on their shoulders plus gas masks strapped around their necks. After a two-hour delay, we finally said good-bye to Plymouth and England and were now embarked on a frightening yet historic journey.

The coast of France emerging in the afternoon mist seemed to be as a peaceful and tranquil landfall until Army amphibious vehicles met our approach. Then, these land/water carriers (LCI's or Landing Craft, Infantry) slid up to us shipside and rope netting ladders were deployed. Our ship was evacuated in record time as our men scrambled down these rope ladders into awaiting landing crafts.

The peaceful-seeming shores of France turned out to be a grisly and shocking sight of dead bodies gently stacked in neat piles waiting for their proper disposal. Destroyed tanks, trucks and vehicles of all kinds along with smashed gliders, abandoned field packs and gas masks lay everywhere. Rifles, machine guns and mortars lay next to dead soldiers who had tried to carry them ashore. The debris of battle lay all around us as evidence of the horror of the Allied assault. Barrage balloons filled the skies protecting our precarious toehold from enemy air attacks. This, we were told, was Utah Beach.

One Soldier's Journey

The soldiers who initially assaulted this beach on D-Day, nine days before, had been launched from landing crafts about eleven and a half miles off shore to avoid the risk of exposing the mother troop ship to German shore batteries. Many of these men washed up on the beach dead, with vomit bags, seasick pills and rosaries clutched in their hands.

Chapter 17

Hedgerows and LT B. B. Walker

Normandy, France
Late June 1944 – Mid-July 1944

Except for the choppy seas, our channel crossing to Utah Beach was actually quite uneventful. As we approached the beach, however, we were amazed to see the hundreds of assorted naval vessels, all waiting off-shore to discharge their troops and back-up military equipment, and shocked at the horrific view of military carnage scattered on the beach as far as the eye could see.

During the early hours of D-Day, the 82nd and the 101st Airborne Divisions were dropped into our VII Corps Sector. After their drop and consolidation, that area was turned over to the 4th, 9th and 90th Infantry Divisions. Their orders were to secure and consolidate the Sainte-Mere Eglise, La Haye du Puits[8] and Hill 84 triangle.

The 79th Infantry Division's mission was to cut off the Cotentin Peninsula and capture the city of Cherbourg, which was to be used as a supply port. The 79th was first committed to combat on that mission on June 19, 1944. Following artillery bombardments and air support, Cherbourg surrendered on June 25, 1944.

---

[8] On 17 June 2002, after I had completed this book, I received word from the US Department of State that I had been awarded the Croix de Guerre with Palm by the Republic of France on 14 January 1949. The entire regiment and all others who had helped recapture France received this award, albeit 53 years late.

One Soldier's Journey

On June 27, the 79th Division turned south under the command of the VIII Corps and relieved elements of the 90th Division, which had been badly mauled. They then had to advance over the most difficult terrain of hedgerows ever encountered in warfare. It was at this point, I joined Company L, 315 Infantry Regiment, 79th Infantry Division as First Lieutenant, Executive Officer, second in command under First Lieutenant Tom Carroll from Omaha, Nebraska.

To explain more about these terrible hedgerows, this sector of Normandy consisted of apple orchards, farmlands, small truck gardens and dairy cattle. Many centuries ago, instead of fences, each field was defined and outlined by four- to six-foot mounds of dirt with shrubbery on top. These fields were about half the size of a football field and proved to be excellent fortifications for the German defense troops. German troops would hollow out and fortify strong points along these hedges with automatic "burp gun" fire with devastating results. Consequently, attacking these hedges from the front was almost suicidal, so considerable mortar and artillery support would be employed during our assault. In order to zero in on these German positions, extremely close fire from our support artillery would be necessary. As a result, in many instances, a "short round" sometimes fell within our assault group wounding and killing many of our own friendly forces.

One unique and strange thing about combat during the war was that neither the Germans nor the Allied armies cared much about attacking and fighting after nightfall. While we fought in France, we had double daylight saving time, which meant that it usually remained daylight until 11:00 p.m. Then, as darkness set in, each side would "dig-in" two-man foxholes and have a system of 50% alert[9] at all times. Each side would usually initiate reconnaissance patrols, probing each other's lines in order to determine the strength and location of the enemy.

The French Resistance fighters, identified by the letters "FFI"[10] on their armbands, were a big help to the Allied forces in locating enemy soldiers. These men and women were fractured units of the French army who were working clandestinely with the Allies. They kept our attacking troops informed of the location of German artillery, German troop strength, German strong points of

---

[9] Fifty percent of personnel would remain on duty and alert, while the other fifty percent slept or rested.
[10] Forces Francaises de la Interieur

One Soldier's Journey

defense and the location of areas called ammunition dumps where explosives might be stored. These brave resistance fighters were invaluable and contributed greatly to our initial success in Normandy. It was quite amusing that they always had ample quantities of calvados with them. This was an extremely potent alcoholic form of applejack. It was home distilled and fermented, and they were most eager to share it with our troops. We found that the alcoholic proof was sufficient to ignite and heat our C-rations over a calvados flame.

During the hedgerow fighting and during that hot July summer of 1944, enemy artillery, automatic machine pistol and machine gun fire were devastating to our troops. In early July 1944, Lieutenant Tom Carroll became a casualty, was evacuated and I assumed command of Company L.

My designated job during this period in early July was that of First Lieutenant, Company Commander, Company L, 3rd Battalion, 315 Regiment, 79th Infantry Division. My job responsibilities actually called for the rank of Captain. However, due to the fact that we were receiving so many replacement captains and second lieutenants from the States, my Battalion Commander decided to use these new replacements in the battlefield rather than risk the lives of the more experienced officers. We soon found out, however, as a result of their inexperience in the field, the replacement captains and lieutenants didn't last very long.

Whenever a new captain arrived, I would be demoted to Executive Officer or Second in Command, and he would take over as the Company Commander. One of the new captains that appeared one day was a university-trained ROTC graduate, all spit and polish, seemingly overwhelmed by his own importance. Upon his arrival, I was demoted to Second in Command. Despite my reassignment, which naturally bothered me a little bit, I quickly offered my help, advice and experience to our new captain. I was abruptly dismissed. Three days later, while we were attacking an enemy strong point, I heard the cry, "Lieutenant Thome! Forward!"

From our mortar positions in the rear, where I was directing supporting fire, I crawled forward and found our new captain dead, a bullet through his helmet and skull. He had led our entire company into an ambush and paid dearly. I again became Company Commander of Company L. My promotion to captain did eventually catch up with me on June 24, 1946, after my discharge from Active duty but while I was still in the Army Reserves, via a letter from the War Department, Adjutant General's Office, Washington, D.C.

One Soldier's Journey

Again leading Company L, I immediately assigned First Lieutenant Bill Priestman, who hailed from Elizabeth, New Jersey, as my Executive Officer. I left intact the assignments of First Platoon Leader, First Lieutenant Ernie Shelton from Brahear, Missouri; Second Platoon Leader, Second Lieutenant Ofie Perkins from Brooks, Georgia; and Third Platoon Leader, Second Lieutenant Jerry Motzko from Little Falls, Minnesota. These very capable platoon leaders would later become instrumental in our attack and capture of a German artillery battery in the village of Remois, France.

My fourth or Weapon's Platoon was assigned to a replacement officer, Second Lieutenant Bartlette Burkard Walker from Mt. Gilead, North Carolina. Lieutenant "B.B." was a unique individual who recently had been graduated from Davidson College, North Carolina, and Officer's Candidate School. B.B. had the dignity, confidence and aplomb of a cigar-smoking Confederate General but with the homespun humor and common sense of an Andy Griffith.

Through many long nights, B.B. and I would sit in my bunker listening for approaching enemy patrols. It was during this time that I learned that his father committed suicide after his mother died in childbirth when B.B. was just an infant. He was then adopted by his very wealthy aunt and uncle who owned the McCrary Hosiery Mills and most of Asheboro, North Carolina.

I also discovered that B.B.'s new wife was pregnant, as was mine. Late one night, somehow, our SCR 300 radio got patched in with the Armed Forces Radio, London. An orchestra was playing "Ruby." B.B. immediately proclaimed, "Wow, if my new baby is a girl, I am going to name her Ruby Lorraine!" Lorraine would be in honor of our Division.

Lieutenant B.B. Walker was an extremely brave and devil-may-care officer and a real leader of men. He was an expert with his 60mm Mortar Squad. In one instance, he dropped a shell into the turret of an attacking German Tiger tank. For this, and for his extreme heroism during other skirmishes, I recommended him to be awarded a Silver Star, an important decoration. He really was the rock upon which I depended.

After the war, B.B. became a millionaire. This began with his bidding on 3,000 pairs of surplus Navy shoes and winning the bid by offering the government thirty-eight cents a pair. B.B. then purchased a station wagon and began to distribute the shoes on consignment to as many general stores and gasoline stations as he could locate throughout North Carolina. His stock of shoes soon became depleted. By shopping around, he discovered a manufacturer in

One Soldier's Journey

Massachusetts who agreed to make shoes for him and attach B.B.'s name to them. Thus, the B.B. Walker Shoe Company was born and became an amazing success. After a short period of time, the B.B. Walker Shoe Company had their own manufacturing plant in Asheboro, North Carolina, and began negotiations to acquire the Wolverine Shoe Company in Michigan.

Many years after the B.B. Walker Shoe Company had been in business, I happened to pick up a copy of the Detroit Free Press. The lead article, "The Tragic Saga of a Speculator Who Played the Futures and Lost," on the Financial Page of the Monday morning edition, dated April 20, 1973, caught my eye. As I read the article, I soon discovered that this story contained information of how my dear army buddy B.B. Walker played the soy bean futures commodities market and lost approximately 7.6 million dollars of his company's funds. Later, I learned that on March 6, 1973, just as dawn broke, searchers found B.B.'s body beside the graves of his father and mother in dew-dipped Sharon Cemetery, atop a rural knoll outside Mt. Gilead, North Carolina. A .22 caliber pistol lay close by.

As we would sit in my bunker during the war, B.B. had described this cemetery to me as being on top of Billy Goat Mountain. He said that if he were killed in combat that is where he would want to be laid to rest. I had told him that I would see to it.

Each day during that hot July summer, I was constantly saddened not only by the death and wounding of the men in our close knit unit but also by the nightly strength reports that listed our daily killed in action (KIA), missing in action (MIA), and seriously wounded in action (SWA). Those reports were forwarded to battalion headquarters each evening as darkness descended. Those reports were always a depressing exercise but were necessary to determine our remaining strength in the battle field. I found it very difficult not to visualize the horror and dismay at the horrible news this brought to the next of kin.

Along with the soldiers, both Allied and German, who were being killed, horses, cattle and other livestock that were grazing in the rural farmlands were sacrificed by being in the wrong place at the wrong time.

On one of those very hot July afternoons, across a hedgerow field over which we had been fighting for several days, a very unexpected and amusing event occurred. Unexpectedly, a German soldier appeared waving a white flag. I immediately sent one of my sergeant volunteers out to meet him mid-field while all hostilities and shooting stopped. This would turn out to be one of the most amazing episodes of my combat experience.

Chapter 18

Hedgerow Country

Lessay, France
Late July 1944

During the course of attacking the Germans, who were heavily defending a field of approximately three acres, a large Holstein cow had been killed and lay mid-field, and was now bloated and rotting in the hot July sun. The stench was overwhelming to both the Americans and Germans. The German soldier's request was simple. "Would you American soldiers agree to a truce so that something could be done to dispose of that damn cow?" I immediately agreed and ordered a Sherman tank forward that was fitted with a bulldozer type front blade. A hole was dug, the cow was buried and all the while this was going on, for the first time, "All was quiet on the Western Front."[11]

After the burial was completed, the white flag came down, and again all hell broke loose. We finally captured that "cow field" after three days of fighting. That night my day's final Strength Report listed six KIA's and twelve SWA's who were evacuated to the rear.

What was quite astonishing to our attacking units was the resistance we encountered from the Germans. Most of them were fanatical and absolutely determined to die for *der_Führer*. An exception to this was when we were confronted by enemy troops who appeared to be of Russian origin. Later,

---

[11] A reference to Erich Maria Remarque's classic book on World War I, written from a German soldier's viewpoint.

One Soldier's Journey

through our means of interrogation, we learned that those poor devils, all wearing German uniforms, had been captured by the Germans on the Russian front and were shipped west in order to blunt and fortify the German coastal defenses. These Russian soldiers appeared to be of Cossack, Tatar or other Russian descent, all natives from the Russian provinces. They were placed in the front lines between the American and German troops. They all knew that if they retreated, they would be shot. In most instances, those poor bedeviled, bewildered and anxious soldiers were eager to surrender. They knew the Germans were just using them as front line fodder.

During the infrequent lulls in battle, we would stop our advance, dig-in and wait for units on our left and right to catch up in order to make our flanks secure. Hopefully, when those little lulls occurred, we would be quartered in shattered buildings in some destroyed village, protected from the cold and rain. Those were the rare times when our cooks, far to the rear, would prepare hot meals and hand carry them, under cover of darkness, to the front line troops. I don't remember how many times this happened. When it did, it was like "manna from heaven." If we were really lucky, our support units back at Quartermasters, who were also assembled far to the rear, would hand-carry down-filled sleeping bags for our comfort. Those were also the times when our next day's rations, water and mail would be delivered.

Sometimes I would receive a packet of five or six letters at one time and I would sit back in my bunker and relish the news from back home, all memories of another world in which I once lived. Our new baby was still on the way, and every facet of the progress of Marian's pregnancy was reported in great medical detail.

News of friends and relatives were most welcome as was new of their problems obtaining tires, gasoline, shoes, butter and meat. Those civilian necessities were all going to our fighting forces and I never heard a complaint from any civilians left behind in regard to the scarcity of those commodities that most folks took for granted before the war.

Included with our nightly rations, we would also occasionally receive assorted PX goodies such as candy bars, cigarettes, toothpaste and other such luxury items. For the good old boys, much to their delight, once in awhile a packet of Red Man, Mail Pouch chewing tobacco or Copenhagen snuff would be thrown in. However, those were rare, almost unheard of, surprises for soldiers fighting on the front lines.

Along with those items, our visitors from the rear would also have information, mostly rumors, about what was happening according to the "big picture," a term frequently used back at Division's rear Command Headquarters. "How are things going on the Russian front?" "How is Monty doing up north and east of us?" And, most important, "When are Ike and Bradley going to unleash Patton and his tanks that are being assembled and hidden among the Normandy apple orchards up north?"

If our situation was such that we were still in the open during those lulls in battle, we kept busy improving our foxholes, writing letters home, while warming our PX packets of Nescafe over "stoves" made from empty tin cans from our C rations that were filled with sand and saturated with calvados. We would again be on 50% alert in case of a sneak German counter attack. While we were in our foxholes, we would attempt to cover ourselves with our raincoats to protect ourselves from the rain and other inclement weather.

As we continued to progress through the hedgerow country, fighting for every inch of French soil, we heard rumblings about considerable activity in and around the apple orchards to our rear. Supply dumps, ammunition dumps and gasoline were being stored and accumulated among the trees. Every day more and more tanks and armored vehicles were being added to the Allied arsenal of reinforcements. Finally, the word was out, General Patton and his 3rd Army were arriving from England, and he was itching for a fight. In the meantime, every night a German reconnaissance plane would fly over our area taking pictures trying to determine what was going on. We just ignored it. We identified him as "bed check Charlie." We never shot at him for fear we might disclose our positions.

By late July, we finally broke out of the hedgerow country and stopped our attack on the high ground north of Lessay, which is on the west coast of the peninsula. Here we reorganized and received replacements for our dead and wounded. The replacements were new, fresh from the States, and green, but were enthusiastic officers and enlisted men. During the month of July, Company L lost a total of 153 men and officers who were either dead or wounded. It was difficult to believe how I had lived such a charmed life, considering all of the bullet and shrapnel holes in my clothing.

Having reached the high ground overlooking the town of Lessay, I immediately established a line of defense by having my men dig-in their two-

One Soldier's Journey

man foxholes with the usual 50% alert around the clock to meet and ward off the anticipated German counter-attacks. During this time, we received incoming, sporadic German artillery fire. We never knew whether this would be followed by an assault from their ground troops.

Strange to say, the front was quite inactive at this time in spite of the constant enemy harassment. I believed that this was due to the pressure being exerted by the English and other Americans on the German forces east from our position. It appeared that the Germans to our front were also ready for a breather. We now had the opportunity to receive our next day's rations, bedrolls and blankets. What luxury! Frequently, the cooks would bring-up a hot meal to us on the front lines. If things were especially quiet, I would send my men, a squad at a time, for a shower located in a safe area to our rear. Our main mission at this time was to maintain binocular observation on the Germans during the daylight and on their recon (reconnaissance) patrols at night.

The Ay River, which was about twenty to thirty yards wide and ran through the town of Lessay, separated us from the enemy. The Germans were obsessed with re-building a bridge that had been destroyed. Their engineers were using wooden planks, beams and logs to accomplish this difficult task. Finally, it was finished. As the German engineers stood by admiring their work, I promptly called back to our artillery and had them "fire for effect." Our 105's and 155's responded and blew their new bridge to smithereens. Just as the smoke cleared, sure enough, those fanatical and obsessed German engineers were right back there, rebuilding their bridge. Again, I called for artillery to blow it apart. This happened three different times before the enemy finally abandoned their project.

Chapter 19

Operation Cobra

Lessay, France
Late July 1944

    During a very welcome pause in our 24-hours of combat, we were finally able to shave and take a bath from the rationed water in our helmets with enough left over to wash our socks. I also realized that I was finally battle tested, and I could now sense when to duck into a foxhole by the whine of an incoming artillery barrage. This only came after having been caught several times in the midst of an enemy shelling. You then began to know just how far away that shell would land.

    I also discovered that after a replacement soldier experienced a couple of weeks of combat and lived through them, his chances of survival would be greatly increased. Many times, though, while checking the men in their foxholes prior to an attack, I would find several men reading their Bibles. I never quite understood the why or the reason. Usually, they would be the first to be killed or wounded.

    My company was a very close knit cadre of grizzly combat soldiers. At full strength, we would have around 150 to 200 men. Due to constant casualties, however, our strength was usually around 100 to 120 savvy soldiers. At that point, I would again have to wait for replacements.

    The differences in the men were puzzling to me. I once estimated that of all the men in my company, only about 30% of them were aggressive enough to engage and destroy the enemy. The remaining men seemed to be there on a rather passive adventure, scared to death, hoping that they would never confront the enemy. If they did, it seemed to me, it would be impossible for them to kill another human being. I often wondered, is that all bad?

While attacking the enemy, we worked with small-scale combat maps, reproduced from aerial photos that identified each road, trail or man-made structure in the line of our advance. With these maps, and with the help of the FFI, our job was made much easier. At company level, we really didn't know too much about what Division, Corps or Army was planning. We only knew that out there in front of us was a hedgerow, a farmhouse or a small French village defended by the Germans that we had to capture, destroy or secure -- or else die trying.

The path of destruction from the shores of Utah Beach to our present and future locations spared no one. There were terrible losses of Allied and German soldiers, as well as French civilians caught up in the advance of our attacks. Dead animals - dogs, cats, rabbits and even chickens, along with horses, cows, goats and sheep - were strewn across the countryside after we passed through, all bloated and rotting in the summer heat.

While resting at Lessay, I finally had the opportunity to inventory and assess the company's casualties and replace, through promotion, the corporals and sergeants we had recently lost in battle. I quickly realized that replacing casualties was a very important morale factor. The troops had no use for a commander who would have a vacancy in his TO (Table of Organization) and not promptly promote from within to fill that vacancy. Frequently, while in a combat situation, I would promote a private to a sergeant by writing his promotion on the back of an empty envelope and sending it back to Battalion Headquarters for approval.

Each infantry company was staffed with six officers, a Company Commander (Captain), an Executive Officer who was second in command and usually a First Lieutenant, and four platoon leaders who were Second Lieutenants. At the height of combat during the past several weeks, I noticed that I had a large incidence of casualties among my lieutenant platoon leaders. Many had been killed or wounded. I soon discovered that my old battle-scarred sergeants would convince my replacement lieutenants that as leaders, they should be out there in front leading their platoons. I finally had to hold a meeting to instruct everyone that those young officers should not be used as forward scouts or decoys. They were to be protected inasmuch as those tactics were fast depleting our officer corps. My men all agreed and things began to settle down.

At Lessay, we finally determined that the battle of the Normandy hedgerows was over, that the German 7th Army had been destroyed and this was Rommel's last battle. Our appraisal turned out to be correct.

Each front-line combat company also included two unarmed, non-combatant soldiers trained by the Medical Corps as medics. They were identified with Red Crosses emblazoned on their armbands and helmets. Those soldiers administered first aid to the wounded, called in stretcher-bearers if needed, and directed the walking wounded to the nearest Battalion Aid station that was supervised by a medical doctor. The medics' equipment consisted of bandages, plasma, morphine ampoules, slings, braces and the ever-present packets of sulfa powder to treat open wounds. After assessing the wounded, the medics would evacuate them to the rear where, depending upon the diagnosis reached by the Battalion Surgeon, an ambulance might be dispatched to evacuate a patient further back to the nearest Army Base Hospital or even back to London or the U.S.

"Where the lead was thick, the brass was usually thin." Occasionally, our Regimental Commander would appear at the front lines with a macho comment such as, "Let's go, men! Do you people want to live forever?" He would then quickly disappear deep within his bunker, far to the rear. Those were the so-called heroes who received most of the credit, the medals and promotions for what the real heroes, the young privates and lieutenants, died for.

There were some real heroes, especially in the eyes of the front line soldiers. They were the L-5 or Piper Cub pilots. Those brave men were German artillery spotters and were in direct communication with our artillery batteries. As they would fly their planes low and in front of our lines to observe German artillery firing at us, they would immediately identify the enemy's coordinates and direct devastating Allied counter fire. Consequently, when those planes would fly overhead, all German artillery would cease firing to prevent revealing their positions. Nevertheless, many of these brave young pilots got shot down behind enemy lines.

On the morning of July 27, 1944, the ground shook with the vibrations of hundreds of heavy bombers passing over our lines, heading south and east. Fighter planes, including P-47's, P-51's and English Spitfires, led the way

One Soldier's Journey

protecting the 1,800 B-17 heavy bombers. The entire sky was filled with aircraft. The magnitude of this operation was awesome. It turned out to be the start of General Bradley's Operation Cobra. The plan was to break out of the hedgerow country in order for General George Patton's Third Army and his tank divisions to be unleashed into the rolling plains of the French countryside. I found out later that this bombing maneuver practically wiped out German General Bayelein's troops and those that remained were either wounded, demoralized or disoriented. They probably also lost a great deal of supplies and equipment.

Sad to say, we also lost men due to the close proximity of our Allied bombing to our front lines. A total of 111 men were killed and 450 of our soldiers were wounded in the area where the bomb drop was made. Killed was our General Lesley McNair, Chief of Army Ground Forces, who had attended the operation as an observer.

But, hold it Nelly! Here comes General Patton, ivory-handled pistols strapped across his belly!

I never did have any direct contact with General Patton, but we were all influenced by his orders. They would originate at his Army Headquarters, proceed through Corps, Division, Regiment, and at the bottom of the command list would be Company L. We all joked about his directives. For instance, once when we were approaching the German border, he ordered that there would be absolutely no fraternization among the American troops and the German civilians. Then, he followed that order up with, "All soldiers entering Germany will be issued condoms." Also, during the Battle of the Bulge when it was impossible to get air support due to the weather, he called in his favorite chaplain and told him to prepare a prayer asking God to clear the skies. He followed this up by telling him, "By God, Chaplain, it damn well better be a good one, or you'll hear it from me." Very shortly thereafter, the skies cleared and our bombing and strafing continued.

Many people accused General Patton of wearing pearl-handled revolvers. This was not true. They had ivory handles. Patton was tough, audacious, daring and bold, yet somewhat religious. He corresponded with his family back in the States and wrote poetry. He was a strange man who loved combat, soldiering, and military history all the way back to the Greek and Roman generals. He was fearless to a fault.

Chapter 20

"Blood and Guts"

Avranches, France, to the Battle of Falaise Gap
Late July 1944 – Mid-August 1944

Patton's Third Army had jockeyed for position while being concealed under the apple trees of Normandy. After the saturation bombing by our 8th Air Force had been completed, Patton and his troops burst out of the hedgerow country like a wild hoard of Cossack cavalrymen. His Fourth and Eighth Armored Divisions fanned out to the south, east and west. His tanks and armored vehicles traveled so fast and covered so much ground that when we broke out of the hedgerows, usually Patton's tank divisions had advanced several kilometers ahead of us.

Then disaster struck. His tanks, which were far out to our front, ran out of gas. He had out-paced his supply line. Consequently, his progress came to a screeching halt. Patton was furious because the Germans now had the opportunity to dig-in and establish strong defensive positions. This resulted in many, many casualties among our supporting infantry troops, including my company and our division. Old "Blood-and-Guts" Patton's entire philosophy and strategy of warfare was, "Attack, attack, attack; move fast; and don't let the enemy dig-in."

This gasoline shortage seemed to last forever before Quartermasters, the Red Ball Express and the Transportation Corps could muster up and replenish Patton's tanks with more gasoline. All during that time the atmosphere was blue

One Soldier's Journey

with Patton's curses. I am certain that many heads did roll because of this military faux pas.

Until the tanks ran out of gas, we really had the Germans on the run. They were confused, bewildered and grouping in isolated pockets of resistance, trying desperately to reassemble. We continued to be amazed at their determination and heroics in spite of our overwhelming advantage.

On the day that Patton's attack began, the 6th and 79th Infantry Divisions were attached to his Third Army. It was our mission to follow this hell-for-broke armor and clean up the many pockets of resistance that Patton's tanks by-passed. The Germans also experienced a fuel shortage, which caused the German Tiger and Panther tanks to become immobile. Consequently, they were deployed as stationary artillery pieces and were used against our attacking ground troops with devastating success.

Of course during that period, our armor losses were also formidable. Nevertheless, our advance was so rapid and the battle lines were so fluid that in several instances we advanced twenty to thirty miles a day, going for thirty-six hours, as we fought for every inch of French soil. Again, we were attempting to comply with Patton's orders, "Move fast and don't let the enemy dig in." This we did and rapidly captured and cleared the towns of Avranches, Pontorson, Fougeres and Laval of all German resistance.

On or about the eighth of August, I received the directive to organize a motorized combat patrol with the mission to enter and secure the town of Le Mans. It had been reported that there was considerable German resistance in that area. I assembled one of my twenty-five man platoons, placed them in a 2½-ton Army personnel carrier and equipped each man with an automatic weapon. I climbed into the lead jeep that was equipped with a driver, a mounted 50-caliber machine gun and one of my sergeants as gunner. While completing our patrol, we maintained radio communication with battalion headquarters to keep them informed of our progress.

When we reached the town square, we quickly discovered that the Germans were not defending the city except for a few die-hard snipers, who were quickly dispatched. My next concern became the outburst of unbridled civilian jubilation and excitement upon our arrival. Our 79th Army Division identification and emblem worn on our helmets and shoulders was the Cross of Lorraine. The emblem was a shield with a cross of double horizontal bars on a blue background. Lorraine is an historic French province. When the French civilians saw this emblem, they all thought that we were a French division sent to liberate their city. When they discovered that we were American troops, the frenzy became even greater. White sheets of surrender and French tri-colored flags began to appear waving from the rooftops, balconies, windows and storefronts. My men were handed bouquets of flowers, bottles of wine, baked goods, and I'm sure that other favors were offered by the ecstatic French mademoiselles as well.

I finally received assurances from the French Resistance fighters that the city was indeed secure and that it was under their control and that the Germans, except for a few fanatics, had abandoned the city. It was now my challenge to round up my patrol while battalion headquarters crackled over my radio wondering what was going on. To buy time, I radioed back that I was having my men check the bridges for demolition charges and that things were under control. Little did headquarters know of the "amour courtois" going on between the American GI's and those hospitable and passionate French ladies.

After Le Mans, our battle-tested division fanned out far and wide, north across the fields and meadows of France. We destroyed and smashed villages, towns, schools and churches in our path, all occupied and used by the Germans to stop our progress. Moving swiftly, within seventy-two hours our Division had traveled 180 miles across the battlefields of World War I.

As our persistent assault against the enemy positions became more and more ruthless and aggressive, it seemed to me that the odds of survival began to diminish dramatically. Already, I had evidence of bullet holes in my field jacket and artillery shrapnel had shot off the heel of one of my combat boots. Despite many near death encounters, I remained ineligible for a Purple Heart because I remained devoid of a bleeding wound.

As we moved north with the 5th Armored Division on our flanks, we continued our devastation of killing, wounding and capturing the enemy, while caring for our own wounded and identifying our dead. Our goal was to meet up with the British in order to encircle what remained of the German Seventh Army.

That encirclement was completed in the vicinity of Le Mele-sur-Sarthe. Here, on August fourteenth, our division, teaming up with fighter/bomber units from the 9th Air Force, destroyed hundreds of enemy vehicles, horses, artillery pieces, horse-drawn wagons of rations, ammunition and equipment. Mile after mile, dead German soldiers and their personal equipment littered the roads from

One Soldier's Journey

being caught in our incessant bombing and strafing; a complete military disaster on their part. The German Army was trapped and it was totally impossible for them to escape. The terrible death and destruction in this area were complete and sickening. This encounter with the German Army became historically known as the "Battle of Falaise Gap." I was there and saw it all.

Prior to Falaise, Operation COBRA, planned and plotted by General Bradley, and executed by the flamboyant, audacious, and sometimes brutal, 3rd Army Commander, General George S. Patton, had also turned out to be a brilliant military campaign. It had totally confused and disorganized the methodical defensive plans of the Wehrmacht.

Even though the battle to close the Falaise Gap was devastating to the Germans, as proven by the awesome sight of dead soldiers who had been killed while retreating on bicycles or on foot, thousands of German troops did escape with most of their equipment only to re-trench further to the east and again engage us in a fanatical defense of their motherland. This was all due to the failure of British Field Marshal Montgomery's attempt to close the northern flank of our entrapment. As a result of Montgomery's lack of aggressiveness and his apparent lack of boldness as a commander, General Patton developed an intense disrespect for Montgomery's ability to lead troops. Patton forever blamed Montgomery for his failure at Falaise. Patton's disdain for Montgomery remained throughout the war, two giant egos that constantly clashed.

Because of the 79th Division's battle reputation and success at Falaise, Normandy, Cherbourg and the hedgerows of Western Europe, we were quickly identified as an effective attack division. Consequently, we would be called on wherever trouble erupted. As we later would continue to head eastward across France, many times we were ordered to shift quickly north or south from the Belgian border to the Ruhr Valley and then down to Alsace then north again to Luxembourg, depending upon where the strength of the German defenses lay. It seemed like we were constantly on the move, walking, riding on trucks or hanging on tanks to relieve our tired and aching feet. Many times we would walk twenty or thirty miles a day in order to stop some enemy penetration. After that, we might be transported fifty to a hundred miles in one day to prevent some other division from becoming outflanked. As a result, exhaustion and casualties mounted and morale soon became a serious problem for us as well as for all front-line commanders.

One Soldier's Journey

Our infantry soldiers often contrasted their hardships with those of the Air Corps personnel who would fly a certain number of assigned missions and then be relieved to return to the States for rest and rehabilitation (R&R). The difference was that an infantry soldier was expected to fight until death or until he was wounded and evacuated from combat. Because of this difference in the military services, every soldier on the front lines hoped that he would be hit with that "million dollar" flesh wound, something minor that would remove him from the front and back to an evacuation hospital far to the rear.

Chapter 21

Sitting Ducks

Remois, France
Late August 1944 – September 15, 1944

After the Battle of Falaise Gap, we continued our march north and finally crossed the Seine at Mantes-Gassicourt. That was the situation I was in when I received the wonderful news via cable, **"JAMES MICHAEL THOME born August 23, 1944 at 2:20 PM, 8 lbs., 7 oz. Mother and child doing well."** I was ecstatic with that news and more than ever was I determined to survive in order to see my son and to congratulate, praise and thank his mother for bearing that ordeal alone.

On August 30, we experienced a breakout under the First Army, XIX Corps. We then again became motorized and headed for the Belgian frontier. We crossed the Belgian border on September first and second, the first American division to do so in World War II. We later discovered that we were directed north in order that General LeClerc[12], a French division commander, could continue his attack and, for political purposes, capture Paris.

From September second to the fifth, our division waited for new orders at our assembly area near Sameon on the Franco-Belgian border. The next day, we started south to rejoin Patton's Third Army and the XV Corps. We were needed to help put out another fire.

---

[12] General Jacques Phillippe LeClerc, Commander, French Second Armored Division

One Soldier's Journey

    As we advanced south, small rural farmlands lay in our path destroyed, caught in the cruel devastation of war. Farmhouses were usually constructed of stone or brick with an attached shed or barn, which housed the owners' cows, chickens and other farm livestock. The wealth of each farm could usually be gauged by the size of the manure pile adjacent to the main building (put there to provide warmth to the house). Indoor plumbing was a rare curiosity, and in a pinch any bush, shrub or tree would serve as an inelegant substitute for a tiled bathroom for both men and women. A collection of these farms would make up a small village. Now, most of them lay in ruins, the buildings damaged or destroyed, the animals dead, and the people starving.

    As we advanced, the French villagers would rise up and attack any retreating German occupation troops. The French knew that if the Germans defended a village they captured, we would call upon our heavy artillery and our P47 fighter/bomber planes to destroy that village. In the course of such action, we would not only kill the enemy; we would devastate the surrounding farms, churches and schools. We welcomed and appreciated the French cooperation even though it was just self-preservation on their part.

    During the cool nights of September with their frequent and chilling rains, I would diligently study my battle maps with my platoon leaders to determine if a town or village lay in our sector of attack. Upon discovering one, I would immediately instruct my lead platoons that the town or village would become our initial objective. If we captured it, we could occupy an abandoned building, out of the weather and not in a wet, muddy and soggy foxhole. We never had any trouble commandeering shelter from the French. Usually the houses, barns and sheds were unoccupied, the residents having fled from the onslaught of war. The Germans had the same idea. Consequently, as the weather continued to turn bad, we both fought bitterly for these shelters.

    On September 14, 1944, the little village of Remois lay in our attack sector. It was being defended by German ground troops along with a formidable artillery battery. I was given the order to attack, capture, and perhaps destroy the German battery since it was impeding the advance of our entire regiment.

    I held a meeting with my platoon leaders, Lieutenants Shelton, Perkins, Motzko, Priestman and Walker. After a map reconnaissance, we determined the approximate location of the German guns, hidden and camouflaged in the trees and shrubbery about 500 meters to our front. I warned them if these artillery

One Soldier's Journey

pieces were defended by ground troops and those troops were a unit of the elite Waffen SS[13], they probably would be armed with Schmeisser *machinepistoles*.

These guns were rapid-fire, mobile personnel weapons, which were behind the impressive combat power of the German Army. When this was the case, the usual German tactic would be to open fire on attacking troops with devastating power, pin them down, and while we were pinned down and immobile, the Germans would adjust their mortar or artillery fire and pound the Allies with high explosives. It is almost impossible to adjust artillery fire on moving targets. That is the reason the Germans used their machine pistols and rifle fire to pin their enemy down.

I deployed my company in a skirmish line with Lieutenant Shelton's platoon on the left, Lieutenant Perkins' platoon on the right and Lieutenant Motzko's platoon in reserve. Lieutenant Walker supported us with machine gun and mortar fire. Lieutenant Priestman followed along with Lieutenant Walker ready to take my place in case I became a casualty.

From the very start of our attack, the platoons of Lieutenant Shelton and Lieutenant Perkins were pinned down by intense machine gun and automatic rifle fire. As they hit the ground looking for cover, German mortars zeroed in on them and proceeded to batter the men terribly. As I recognized our predicament, determined that my men were not to become sitting ducks for the German artillery, I jumped up and shouted, "Let's move!" And, move we did, firing our rifles as we all charged forward. We captured the German artillery battery consisting of four 75mm guns and about thirty German soldiers supporting them. The Germans were indeed a unit of the Waffen SS, as I had suspected.

Due to losses from previous skirmishes, my platoons were all under-strength. Our attacking force consisted of approximately 126 American soldiers. Our losses at the battle of Remois included a total of fourteen killed and eleven wounded. By charging the German's position, I am positive that I saved more soldiers than if we had remained pinned down with artillery shells exploding all around us. It could have been much worse. For this action, I was awarded the Bronze Star. The Citation reads:

---

[13] Literally "Armed SS"

FIRST LIEUTENANT, JAMES L. THOME, 01313514, INFANTRY, 315TH INFANTRY, UNITED STATES ARMY, FOR MERITORIOUS ACHIEVEMENT IN ACTION AGAINST THE ENEMY ON 14 SEPTEMBER 1944, IN FRANCE. WHEN ENEMY ARTILLERY CONCENTRATIONS ARRESTED THE ATTACK ON REMOIS, LIEUTENANT THOME DELIBERATELY AND WITHOUT REGARD FOR HIS PERSONAL SAFETY, EXPOSED HIMSELF

TO ENEMY ARTILLERY AND INTENSE SMALL ARMS FIRE IN ORDER TO RALLY HIS MEN AND LEAD THEM FORWARD TO THE ATTACK. HIS EXEMPLARY COURAGE AND BRILLIANT LEADERSHIP REFLECT GREAT CREDIT ON THE ARMED FORCES OF THE UNITED STATES. SIGNED: KRAMER THOMAS, COLONEL, CHIEF OF STAFF.

Major General Wyche, our Division Commander, observed my actions while he stood on high ground overlooking the battle scene. He personally instructed our Battalion Commander to award me the Bronze Star[14]. On

---

[14] **Criteria for Award**: a. The Bronze Star Medal is awarded to any person who, while serving in any capacity in or with the military of the United States after 6 December 1941, distinguished himself or herself by heroic or meritorious achievement or service, not involving participation in aerial flight, while engaged in an action against an enemy of the United States; while engaged in military operations involving conflict with an opposing foreign force; or while serving with friendly foreign forces engaged in an armed conflict against an opposing armed force in which the United States is not a belligerent party. b. Awards may be made for acts of heroism, performed under circumstances described above, which are of lesser degree than required for the award of the Silver Star. c. Awards may be made to recognize single acts of merit or meritorious

One Soldier's Journey

September 15, 1944, our whole division was assembled at Charmes to support the bridgehead and to secure the east bank of the Moselle River. My thoughts continued to be with my wife and newborn son and the progress being made by the Russian troops on the eastern front. Our worst was yet to come.

---

service. The required achievement or service while of lesser degree than that required for the award of the Legion of Merit must nevertheless have been meritorious and accomplished with distinction.

Chapter 22

Combat Fatigue

Foret de Parroy – Luneville, France
September 1944

Nervous exhaustion, best described as "combat fatigue" in World War II, or as "shell shock" in World War I, began to become more and more evident and a serious concern among commanders of front-line ground troops. This problem, plus evidence of several incidents of self-inflicted wounds, began to define the terrible physical and mental pressures our soldiers were experiencing.

These incidents would usually occur late at night while the troops were "on-line" in their 50% alert foxholes anticipating an early morning attack. One of the men would crawl out of a foxhole under the pretense of relieving himself. Shortly thereafter, a shot would sound, followed by the call, "Medic!" The injured soldier would be treated in the field and then evacuated to the Battalion Aid station. He most likely would have a grazing wound to the arm, leg or the fleshy part of his thigh. Within a day or two, I would receive a memo from the medics requesting that I should conduct an investigation to determine if the wound was the result of an intentional act or an accident.

Whether a soldier's wound was intentional or accidental was almost impossible to prove or disprove. If my response to an inquiry had been that the wound was "intentional," the outcome of the investigation would be devastating to the young soldier in question. Undoubtedly, he would receive a dishonorable discharge, forfeit all pay and allowances due, have to pay for all medical care and treatments, and would lose all future veteran benefits. I always considered

One Soldier's Journey

that, as time went by, the soldier would realize what he had done, and the shameful guilt he would feel in the future would be punishment enough. In my compassion, I always reported back, in every instance, these were accidents. I was acutely aware that old "Blood and Guts" Patton would never have agreed.

During those troubling times, an experience that I will never forget occurred with one of my young soldiers. This young man came from a small town north of Boston. He was drafted in spite of having a wife and three small children. Early one morning, he came to me and said that he just found out (mail call) that his wife had been diagnosed with uterine cancer and that immediate hospitalization and surgery were necessary. "Please, Lieutenant, would it be possible for me to go home at this time in order for me to be with her and the children?"

I told him to contact his doctor, the Red Cross and perhaps his clergyman for verification and then I would apply for his emergency furlough. The required letters were promptly cabled back. I then immediately approved his furlough back to the States and forwarded the furlough request back through channels. Battalion and Regimental Headquarters agreed. Division Headquarters returned my request stamped, "Disapproved." Three days later, this young soldier was shot three times by a German burp gun and died next to me. We were less then 10 yards apart.

Later that night, after my Company had dug-in to defend our position against enemy counter attacks, and after I had requested protective artillery concentrations in front of our lines, I crawled into the shadows of my front-line dugout. Through curses, I cried for that young soldier, his widow and his three little children. I would cry again soon.

Our division continued to range far and wide in stubborn and bitter combat mopping-up operations that extended along the Siegfried Line from Metz south to Nancy and along the Meurthe River line. Along the way, we wiped out enemy garrisons at Poussay, Soissons, Lesmont, Joinville and Neufchateau, finally capturing Luneville on September 24, 1944.

At Luneville, our mission was expanded for us to clear out the vast wooded area east of the city, identified on our battle maps as the "Foret de Parroy." Reconnaissance indicated that the enemy was holding the forest in strength and the "sound and flash" people back at our artillery units reported considerable concentrations of the enemy in the east. So what! Our confidence had been heightened because our division was promised a heavy bombing run by the B-17's from the XIX TAC (Tactical Air Command) prior to our attack. Hopefully that would neutralize the Germans hiding in their fortified bunkers.

What we didn't anticipate was poor weather, which canceled the scheduled aerial bombardment. Our ground attack jumped off anyway at 0700 hours. As usual, Company L was one of the lead companies that charged into the foray.

Our attack turned out to be a disastrous nightmare. My company and our battalion suffered more soldiers killed, wounded, self-inflicted wounds, combat fatigue, mental breakdowns and desertions than at any other time in my combat experience. I'm certain that fighting in this dense wooded area contributed to our difficulties. The enemy would fire artillery shells at us with super quick detonating fuses. They would explode immediately when a branch or twig was hit followed by an explosive air burst over our heads. A foxhole offered no protection.

I would attempt to maintain contact with my platoons by using army walkie-talkies, which were hand-held radio devices. They seldom worked. Due to our close proximity to the enemy, I couldn't shout instructions to my men or apply voice commands. Consequently, we inched along, yard by yard, sometimes employing hand-to-hand combat to fight our way along. If we advanced 10 to 20 yards a day, we considered ourselves successful. Fortunately, we had our own artillery support. In many instances, however, map coordinates were misread by our artillery observers that resulted in "short" rounds falling on us, which only added to the horror of our situation.

Frequently, in the dead of night, we would hear the cry of "Help!" forward of our front lines. The Germans would use this tactic as a ploy to fool our medics. If the medics responded to these false cries for help, they would be shot. On one occasion, from dusk to midnight, we heard a German in front of us screaming in pain. We all wanted to help him but we were afraid that this might be just another deception. Finally, a shot was heard and the screaming stopped. The next morning, one of my sergeants crawled up to my bunker and said that he had shot a German who had his leg blown off and a hole in his chest. A terrible measure to take, but it prevented my company from having a massive mental breakdown.

"Why did you do that terrible thing, Sergeant," I had asked. He responded, "Lieutenant, he was my prisoner and he was trying to escape." I said

One Soldier's Journey

nothing in reply but later, through the Division Headquarters grapevine, I heard that the Inspector General's Department from Army Headquarters was going to investigate Lieutenant Thome's Company L because he was shooting prisoners. That never came about.

The situation in the Foret de Parroy became so hairy that our regimental commander, a lieutenant colonel and a career officer, never left his bunker. He would pee in his helmet and direct some private to dispose of it. The private was eventually promoted to corporal. The colonel received some choice assignments before he retired. Thus were the twists and turns of warfare.

Chapter 23

Despair

Bayon and Saverne, France
October 1944

After two more weeks of fighting, the enemy was finally driven off. On October 9, 1944, the 44th Division relieved our badly mauled 79th Division. This was our first break from combat in 128 days. We reorganized in Bayon, France, which is a small town south of Luneville. There, we began to receive replacements for our killed and wounded.

My men were quartered in a large rail warehouse on the Rue de Gare (literally "street by the railroad") in Bayon, where they were provided with beds of straw along with blankets and bedrolls. I was assigned a billet with a bedroom in a private home and was supplied with a down comforter, pitcher with wash basin and even a potty under my bed. What luxury! Yet during the following few nights, despite my sumptuous surroundings, I would have continuous nightmarish experiences of hearing imaginary German artillery bursting over my head.

Our mail now finally had a chance to catch up to us after our three to four weeks of isolation and fighting in and around the Foret de Parroy. My first mail consisted of an unusually large packet of letters from my wife, who was now a new mother, and from friends and relatives in the States. Anxious to receive news regarding the progress and welfare of my new son, I excitedly tore open the first letter from my wife. To my shock and dismay, it contained a vivid description of my baby's funeral!

One Soldier's Journey

I just couldn't comprehend how something like this could have happened, especially back in the States, supposedly a safe place with doctors and hospitals instantly available. I just had lost sixty-two young soldiers, either killed or wounded in the Foret de Parroy. This I could understand. But to lose my beautiful and healthy young son while in the safety of his loving mother, caring relatives and readily available medical help was impossible to rationalize. I cried alone with those letters in my hand, spotted with tears. I wondered how in God's name could that have happened.

I quickly arranged my wife's correspondence in sequence according to the dates on the postmarks. I discovered that our new son had developed a mild case of diarrhea after being discharged from the hospital. It further developed into a more serious infantile diarrhea that failed to respond to the usual home remedies. James Michael Thome was finally admitted to the Emergency Department of Blodgett Memorial Hospital in Grand Rapids, Michigan. He died there on September 30, 1944, of malnutrition and dehydration, one week after my 25th birthday. He was five weeks old.

My emotions, consumed by frustration, then depression and finally exhaustion, were almost overwhelming. Alone and isolated, I cried. I cried for my baby, James Michael. I cried for the sixty-two men who were either killed or wounded in the Foret de Parroy. I cried for the soldier who was denied a leave so that he could be with his cancer stricken wife and three small children. I cried for all the little innocent French children who were now orphans as a result of this damnable and crazy war. From the depths of my despair, I wondered where all this would end. I wondered whose side God was really on.

I am certain that if General Patton had been around then, he would most certainly have slapped me back to my senses. Soon, I began to remember once again the seriousness of my mission and how important it was for me to provide the leadership and direction my young soldiers so desperately needed at this time. I knew that I had to carry on despite my agonizing personal loss.

After our rest in Bayon, our orders were to continue our attack and pursue the enemy east in the direction of Saverne, which lay in the beautiful and wooded foothills of the Vosges Mountains. During our advance, we were embroiled in bitter fighting with the Germans. We were most anxious to determine the strength and composition of the enemy we were facing in order to develop an effective offensive strategy. We decided that in the instances when the enemy defenses were light, our pursuit must be hot and heavy. Many times,

One Soldier's Journey

we would hitch rides aboard Sherman tanks to pursue the enemy as they withdrew. At times, there would be a dozen or so infantrymen clinging to a mobile tank or tank destroyer, thankful for the lift.

On one such occasion, as our column was advancing down a dusty French road, an artillery round from a German 88mm gun exploded in front of our lead tank from a field about 200-300 yards in the rear of a house facing the road (front). Immediately, we all dismounted from the tanks, on which we had hitched rides, and established a defensive skirmish line not knowing the strength of the enemy facing us or what their intentions were. I finally identified the gun's location and instructed Sergeant Bill Van Dyk to set up his mortars shielded by the house that stood between the German battery and us. I immediately gave the command to commence lobbing mortar shells on the German position. While Sergeant Van Dyk was adjusting his fire, while he was still in front of the house, I saw one of the German gun crew depress his muzzle and aim his gun at the house where our mortar crew was positioned. One armor-piercing shell (the dreaded 88mm) was fired. It entered the rear of the house and exited out the front, killing Sergeant Van Dyk and his entire mortar crew.

At the same time, the Germans initiated a counter attack, which we managed to repulse as darkness set in. That evening when our daily strength report was filled out, my First Sergeant, John Haines, listed Sergeant Van Dyk and the rest of his crew as MIA (Missing in Action). We all knew that they had been killed but we could not list them as KIA (Killed in Action) unless we could prove, by means of positive identification, they had died. The next morning, we regained some lost ground, killed and captured the German forces, destroyed their artillery and positively identified our dead mortar crew. That evening we listed them all on our strength report as KIA.

Sergeant Van Dyk was from my hometown, Grand Rapids, Michigan. After the war, I contacted the Van Dyk family. They were amazed that I was with Bill when he was killed. On a Sunday afternoon, amid twenty or so of his relatives, I described exactly how, when and where Bill was killed.

The family was first notified that something had happened to Bill when the War Department sent them a telegram informing them that Sergeant Bill Van Dyk was an MIA. They did not receive a "Killed in Action Report" until several weeks later.

One Soldier's Journey

After I had explained the circumstances of Bill's death to his family and answered their many questions, they expressed enormous relief to me because now they could have closure. They had been hoping against all hope that Bill was still alive somewhere in Europe, perhaps even a German prisoner. Now they could accept his death with dignity and compassion. They expressed their heartfelt thanks to me for having contacted them.

Chapter 24

The Ugly Americans

Strasbourg, Colmar and Mulhouse, France
October 1944 – November 1944

  After Saverne, we continued our advance to Strasbourg and then south to Colmar and Mulhouse on the Rhine River. We finally dug in and established a hold position in an area that overlooked the river. Lieutenant "Crash" Gagnon, a professional wrestler in civilian life, was assigned to me from our Division artillery as a front line observer. His mission was to direct artillery fire at targets of opportunity that might appear on the other side of the river. To my amazement, directly ahead across the river stood a three story building with "THOME PAPIER COMPANY" emblazoned across its front. I informed Crash that the "THOME PAPIER COMPANY" building was "off limits" to his 155mm howitzers because those people were my relatives and they had five beautiful daughters. He agreed and that building remained unscathed.

  (Actually, this big fat lie might well have been the truth! My great, great grandparents did in fact come from that area of Germany, and it is quite possible that the Thome Papier Company may have been owned by relatives. And, who knows how many beautiful daughters they had. Wouldn't they be surprised if they knew the cause of their building being spared!)

  As the fall days of October and November arrived, daylight hours began to shorten. Consequently, our hours of living in the cold and miserable dampness of foxholes and protective ground dug bunkers were greatly extended since there was an unofficial understanding between the German and American armies not

One Soldier's Journey

to fight after nightfall. Therefore, as we advanced eastward and into the more populated areas along the Ruhr Valley and along the Rhine River, both the Americans and Germans would fight fiercely to capture the protective cover of buildings for the night rather than endure the cold and dampness of dark and uncomfortable foxholes.

Many behavioral problems began to surface among our troops. As our persistent attacks of the Germans began to overrun more populated areas, deliberate looting of valuables found in captured, destroyed or unoccupied civilian homes began to occur. I firmly believe this was the direct result of an extension of our Army's APO "franking" mail service, which allowed packages to be sent to the States, postage and duty-free.

The first packages that were sent home under this system were usually souvenirs or mementos of the German Army and Nazi Party. Nazi flags, Nazi posters removed from schools and public buildings, medals and decorations removed from German prisoners, and in some instances, Luger pistols, holsters, ceremonial swords and an endless array of German army equipment classified as memorabilia were all sent to the States as souvenirs. All such items were mailed postage and duty-free.

Eventually, the horrible realization dawned on me that many of those "souvenir" packages being sent home to the States postage and duty-free were actually the precious possessions of German and French civilians who had abandoned their homes during an artillery bombardment. Before they could return home, our American GIs would "liberate" or loot any item of value they could get their hands on. The "loot" usually consisted of sterling silver, jewelry, crystal, needlework, and anything else of value that they could grab, snap-up and mail home as a souvenir. This shameful activity was so wide-spread among our troops that it became almost impossible to control or police.

One typical example of how this rampage of looting by the American GIs affected the civilians whose homes had been pilfered concerned an elderly Frenchman who suddenly appeared out from the rubble of a bombed-out country home. He approached me, gesturing wildly, and was quite obviously very agitated. After I calmed him down, I discovered that one of our soldiers had stolen his beautiful black fur stovepipe hat that he wore only at weddings, funerals and baptisms. He was absolutely disconsolate. As we were talking, there appeared in a cloud of dust across the horizon a jeep driven by a soldier wearing the old Frenchman's silk hat. It was long gone and we both knew it. I couldn't keep from smiling, but inside I was sickened.

In Stephen E. Ambrose's *Citizen Soldiers*, he states that there were thousands of ordinary criminals in the European Theater of Operations (ETO). Many were caught and court martialed, sentenced to the stockade, or in cases of rape or murder, sentenced to death. I am positive that whatever number Mr. Ambrose arrived at, that number could easily be tripled. I can assure you that according to my experience in the war, the American GI was certainly not our country's best ambassador.

During this period, our mission was to clear the enemy out of Strasbourg and then proceed south to Colmar and Mulhouse, cleaning out German strong points along the way. Fighting was sporadic inasmuch as the German Army was in retreat and wildly disorganized. Finally, upon reaching Mulhouse, we were placed in division reserve for five days in order to regroup. Every morning, during those five days, each platoon would report from one to five men missing and apparently AWOL. None of us could understand what was happening to our Company L until Bart Walker and I looked over a battle map back at our Battalion Command Post and discovered that we were only 20 kilometers from the Swiss boarder. It then dawned on us that our missing soldiers were sneaking across the Swiss frontier where they would be interned for the duration of the war.

One of our men was apprehended and returned to Army control before reaching Switzerland. He was promptly charged with desertion in the face of the enemy. At a general court-martial he was found guilty and sentenced to death by a firing squad. After his sentence, he was removed to a disciplinary barracks in the south of France where he remained until higher headquarters could review his sentence. Later, his sentence was reduced to six months confinement. He was then dishonorably discharged, walked over to another desk and reinducted with a new serial number and with a clean record. He was a new soldier and his past was forgiven. Although desertion was punishable by death by a firing squad, I'm aware of only one sentence actually being carried out during WWII.

The availability of alcohol caused another severe behavioral problem among our troops. Wine, calvados, and later schnapps, were easily obtained from the French in appreciation of our liberation efforts. When supplies dwindled and were not readily available, our armored troops would position an M-1 tank at

One Soldier's Journey

the front entrance of an abandoned so-called party or liquor store and fire a 76mm shell. After the door would be blown open, the liquor store would be immediately over-run by frantic, thirsty GI's who would be overburdened with the looted caseloads of all types of liquor they were attempting to carry off. The result of this, of course, would lead to more discipline problems among our troops, more looting, rape, and other incidents of misconduct.

As the bitter cold nights of November began to settle in, another problem began to develop among our fighting forces. It turned out to be serious and sometimes self-inflicted. Its name was *trench foot*.

Chapter 25

Trench Foot

Bischwiller and Haguenau, France
December 1944

If assigned to an infantry combat division, a soldier could easily learn how to avoid risky enemy combat. It did not take very long since there were many assorted selections on the avoidance menu. Combat fatigue - either real or faked; a self-inflicted wound; Section Eight, mentally unfit - either real or faked; a transfer through political connections; AWOL; out-and-out malingering; and trench foot - one with the most serious of consequences - were just some of the choices that could be made.

Trench foot was actually a misnomer. It had nothing to do with trenches; unless the bottom of a foxhole could be called a trench. Trench foot was caused by standing in your foxhole wearing inadequate leather combat boots that would soak up icy-cold water and then freeze, shrinking the leather tops and thong laces that would then constrict blood flow to the feet, especially the toes. Gangrene would set in as a result of the impaired circulation, and in some instances amputation of toes and part of a foot would become necessary. A soldier would be evacuated to an aid station when he was diagnosed with trench foot. Initially, he might consider it to be the "million-dollar" wound until he became aware of how serious his self-inflicted wound really was and how permanent the consequences.

Certainly, I would like to emphasize that not all trench foot victims resulted from intentional or deliberate misbehavior. Most were innocent victims.

One Soldier's Journey
Yet, many of our soldiers substituted this condition as a welcome alternative to a self-inflicted wound. They felt it was worth the cost to get away from the endless combat and miserable living conditions.

As the cold of winter set in, trench foot became an epidemic. During the winter of 1944-1945, over 40,000 combat soldiers had to be evacuated due to trench foot. The Medical Corps finally decided that each man was to be issued an extra pair of wool socks that were to be changed every day. The extra pair was to be placed under our jackets or coats, next to our bodies to dry out as well as for warmth. Every platoon leader had to check every man in his platoon to see that they complied with these instructions. Any officer whose men continued to develop trench foot was threatened by court martial. Again, because there was such a high incidence of this problem, many of our soldiers were suspected of deliberately causing it. This, I could never prove, nor did I try. But I'm certain that to this day, our government is compensating many trench foot victims who were deliberately responsible for their own condition.

Our next major offensive began on or about December 9, 1944. The 79th was now under VI Corps command. Our mission was to attack northeast along the Rhine River with the objective of breaching the Siegfried Line. Haguenau and Bischwiller were seized and after stubborn enemy delaying tactics, on December 15, 1944, we finally reached the frontier along the Lauter River. At that time, in order to assist us in obtaining our objective, VI Corps decided that we would receive help from one of our airborne divisions. An airdrop was agreed upon and was made about one kilometer to our front. There, they captured the high ground and quickly dug in a defensive position.

Because airborne troops rarely attack on the ground, it was our job to replace their positions and to continue fighting on the ground. Due to the close proximity of the German troops, utmost caution and stealth would be required for us to effectively and secretly replace the airborne troops. It was decided that under darkness, from our assembly area in the rear, two men at a time would move forward and replace two of the airborne soldiers until our entire company was on line and occupying their foxholes. This was an exercise that we anticipated would take the entire night. Upon completion, the plan was to continue our ground attack within the next day or two.

My position in this situation was forward, directing troop traffic and their deployment. Under a bitter cold and moonless night, my first and third platoons, under Lieutenants Shelton and Perkins, did an exceptional job. To my horror, however, coming up the approaching country road appeared Lieutenant Pattock[15], his men in a column of fours with him in the lead, shouting cadence, hut, two, three, four! I was aghast, expecting the Germans to pick up the noise and start shelling our positions at any moment. When I confronted Lieutenant Pattock, I immediately discovered that he was intoxicated, under the influence of perhaps schnapps or calvados. I immediately placed him under arrest. I directed Sergeant "Flattie" Roberts to place him under guard and remove him back to Battalion Headquarters for disposition. As I looked up, I noticed that every man in Lieutenant Pattock's platoon had a smile on his face. They had never before seen one officer arrest another officer. Under these circumstances, they loved what they saw.

Sergeant Roberts took command of the platoon and did a marvelous job. Our replacement of the airborne division was finally completed just before daybreak and after a fifteen-minute barrage by our artillery, we commenced our attack. The Germans had been caught completely off guard.

After Lieutenant Pattock's arrest and removal, I didn't hear any more about him except that he was examined by the division psychiatrist, who declared him unfit for combat duty. He was subsequently transferred to the Transportation Corps and was stationed at some seaport location on the French coast. I also discovered that Lieutenant Pattock was originally trained to be an anti-aircraft gunnery officer. When we obtained air superiority over France, those units had been disbanded and their officers transferred to the infantry. They were neither physically nor mentally prepared for ground combat, nor were they adequately trained for the infantry. I could now understand Lieutenant Pattock's breakdown and empathize with him. I only wished that he had confided in me. I would meet again with Lieutenant Pattock but under much happier circumstances.

Our last advance began to slow down as we were confronted by both passive and still fanatical German soldiers who were either anxious to surrender or who were determined to fight and die for the Fatherland. Our hopes to be home by Christmas soon began to evaporate with rumors of a massive German troop build-up along the front, south of us in the Eiffel or Ardennes sector, east of the Rhine River. The intelligence people back at corps and army headquarters

---

[15] Not his real name.

One Soldier's Journey
scoffed at such a tactic by the Germans. They insisted that because of the ice, snow, fog and mud, a counter offensive at this time would be literally impossible. Little did they know!

Chapter 26

A German Prisoner

Bischwiller and Haguenau, France
December 1944

As expected, homesickness became one of the most significant factors affecting the morale of our troops and it needed to be eliminated quickly. Mail from home was the best remedy for alleviating this problem. Consequently, I sent orders back to our Company clerk, who was stationed back at division headquarters, to make sure that mail delivery to my Company was a top priority unless we were engaged in close combat and within small arms fire. I insisted that our mail be delivered along with our daily food rations. The resulting boost in morale and the smiles on the faces of the men reflected their appreciation of my efforts, which I was pleased to see.

The evening after we captured Haguenau and Bischwiller, I set up our main line of resistance (MLR), which actually became the front line. This is always done when you are in a temporary defensive position and defending against enemy counter attacks. The MLR extends approximately 200 yards from flank to flank depending upon the terrain, and, again, consisting of two-man foxholes spaced a visual distance apart from one another. The flanks are then tied-in with supporting units of soldiers on both the right and left with 50 caliber and 81mm mortars. Additionally, this entire forward area would be supported by 105mm and 155mm artillery that would fire defensive rounds in front of our positions upon my command in the event of a German counter attack. Also for

One Soldier's Journey

our protection, we would establish outposts beyond the MLR that would alert us in case of any enemy infiltration.

The day after we set up the MLR, I received orders from our battalion CO that my company was chosen to send out a small reconnaissance patrol to capture a German prisoner. Our mission was to obtain information from the German soldier regarding the strength, disposition and order of battle of the enemy forces in front of us. The patrol was to be officer-led and was to include not more than three or four soldiers in order to maintain secrecy and total security of the mission. The faces and clothing of the men were to be camouflaged. They were to be equipped with a small rubber boat inasmuch as they had to cross a small stream that flowed between us and the German front. The patrol was to be unarmed in order to avoid a firefight. It was truly a covert exercise with hopes that we could grab a prisoner without being detected.

That same day, I received a replacement second lieutenant and decided that this would be an excellent opportunity for him to distinguish himself as a combat soldier and to demonstrate to the troops what he had learned at the Infantry School at Fort Benning. He became wide-eyed as I revealed my plan and after swallowing hard several times, he finally agreed to "volunteer" and to be the officer in charge of the patrol. He then selected three of my best men to accompany him and they began to prepare for the mission. He checked the timing of the rise and setting of the moon, and ordered a rubber-inflated raft and the proper camouflage clothing from supply.

The tension in the air with regard to this mission was heavy with a sense of foreboding because I couldn't express my concern to the men and had to maintain a positive but guarded demeanor. I really didn't believe this mission would be successful and that it was bound to end up in disaster. I felt that I had ordered these good people to go on a suicide mission. Silently, I prayed that battalion would change their orders and cancel this whole crazy plan.

At 0300 hours, just before the patrol was about to depart from our lines, I received a call on a field telephone from one of our outposts notifying me that a German officer had approached our lines and had surrendered. I immediately held up the patrol, thanked God, and instructed the caller to have the German prisoner escorted back to my command bunker for interrogation.

It turned out that he was a first lieutenant in a German artillery unit that had just been transferred from the Russian front to our area and that his home was about a kilometer to our rear. He told me that before the war he was an

One Soldier's Journey

English teacher in the local high school and he hadn't seen his wife or three little children for three years. He spoke perfect English. Consequently, it gave me the opportunity to offer him a proposition. I told him that if he would give me information on enemy troop strength, morale, deployment of units and perhaps future battle plans, as he knew them, I would allow him to visit his family before turning him over to the prisoner of war and intelligence people. Believing that the war was over and that Hitler was now "kaput," he readily agreed to my terms. After maps were drawn and enemy units were identified, I prepared him for his visit home.

Just a little before daybreak, I had Lieutenant Mueller outfitted with a GI overcoat and pistol belt. I exchanged his German boots for a pair of army shoepacs and placed a GI helmet on his head. One of the corporals and another soldier accompanied Lieutenant Mueller home to a heartwarming and joyous reunion with his family. After about a two-hour sojourn, Lieutenant Mueller returned with his guards to my bunker where we again exchanged equipment and uniforms. I called battalion and told them that we indeed had captured a German prisoner. Lieutenant Mueller and my entire company swore to keep this escapade a deep secret, never to be revealed. It never was. (Until now, that is.)

Lieutenant Mueller certainly did keep up his end of the bargain. He even described how he was captured through the skill of our recon unit led by a brave, young second lieutenant. Our Battalion CO was ecstatic and wanted to know the name of that junior officer who volunteered for such a dangerous mission. When I told him, his response was, "Thome, I want you to write up a Bronze Star medal decoration for that man." That young second lieutenant was the only man I knew who received a Bronze Star medal on his first day in combat for a reconnaissance patrol he never led!

Chapter 27

Horrors of Combat

Wissembourg, France
Mid-December 1944

As we moved north from Haguenau toward Wissembourg, our next objective, progress was agonizingly slow and frustrating. As we advanced, we were not only fighting the cold, frostbite and mud, it also seemed at every bend in the road, a camouflaged German machine gun squad or an 88mm artillery piece was waiting for us.

The German 88mm artillery gun was the most lethal weapon in the enemy's arsenal. Their gunners had the option to shoot either armor-piercing rounds (anti-tank) or high explosive (HE) fragmentary shells (anti-personnel). They could even load them with antiaircraft shells, elevate their muzzles and shoot at our aircraft.

The Allies finally responded to this menace by increasing the size of our tank cannons from 75mm to 76mm and then finally to 90mm. This considerably evened up the score. We also developed the hideous "TOT" ("Time on Target") technique whereby three different artillery batteries, separated by several hundred yards and all with their fuses set, would be fired at the same time. All of their shells would arrive together over the enemy target and all were set for an airburst to occur in unison at approximately ten to twelve feet above the ground. This technique was devastating to the enemy since there was no place to hide and absolutely no protection from our synchronized incoming overhead firepower. Many of the Germans thought our artillery was electrically controlled.

One Soldier's Journey

At the front, each company commander had the luxury of being supported by 60mm mortars with a backup of 81mm mortars from our Battalion Heavy Weapons Company. The 81mm mortar was equivalent to a 105mm-artillery shell. We used this weapon primarily during close-up fighting. Usually, each front line commander had a radio operator at his side in order to maintain contact with the mortar crew in the rear so that an order to adjust firing points could be quickly given. The radioman would have his SCR 300 radio strapped on his back with a microphone in his hand for two-way communications between his front line commander and the mortar crews behind the front line. Since the job of a radioman was crucial to the success of an advance attack against the enemy, he became a vulnerable target who could be easily identified by the radio pack on his back. Knowing this, I would usually try to protect my radio operators by positioning them in the most secure and concealed location that I could find.

On one such occasion when this was done, I learned that the radio operator assigned to me was from my hometown of Grand Rapids, Michigan. His name was Corporal Arthur Ward, and I knew his mother and dad very well. His dad was Peter Ward who worked at the city order desk at Hazeltine and Perkins Wholesale Drug Company. After the war, I learned that Peter and Mrs. Ward were forever grateful to me, believing that through my concern to keep their son protected, his life was spared.

Our deadly artillery guns began to devastate the German infantry so severely that whenever they were in a defensive position, they would frantically work to improve and fortify their foxholes and bunkers. They would gather logs, sod and any other available materials and position them overhead to protect themselves from our incoming artillery shells. Whenever we would over-run one of these fortified, ready-made bunkers, we would consider them to be a captured, deluxe prize of war that we would immediately occupy.

During one of these instances, Lieutenant Harold Friess from Bowling Green, Ohio, and I were plotting-in defensive artillery fire concentrations to protect our lines from threatening German tank attacks. We decided that we would take turns standing "on guard" throughout the night while maintaining radio contact with our artillery forces in case of an enemy attack. With our radio operator and first sergeant, we established our command post, which happened to be in a captured, abandoned and rather deluxe German bunker.

One Soldier's Journey

We decided that Harold would cover the first shift and I would be awakened at 0300 hours to handle the second shift until daylight. About 0100, while Harold was on watch outside the bunker, a salvo of German artillery shells suddenly burst about twenty feet from him. His right arm was severed at the shoulder and his right hip was filled with shrapnel. I immediately rushed to his aid and discovered that the red-hot shrapnel had cauterized and sealed off the blood vessels in his shoulder, which miraculously resulted in a bloodless amputation. I borrowed a scissors from one of our attending medics and cut off the rest of his field jacket along with about three inches of loose skin to complete the amputation. As Harold was placed on a litter to be evacuated, I laid his severed arm across his body and wished him, "Good luck." He looked at me and replied, "Jim, will you please take a look and see if my class ring is still on my finger." It was.

We now realized that after they abandoned a location, the Germans would map the bunker's coordinates, and their artillery would zero in on its new occupants. We never took up housekeeping again in a captured German bunker!

Chapter 28

Battle of the Bulge

Wissembourg, France
Mid-December 1944

    Contrary to the faulty assessment of the German Army's tactical capabilities by our high command, the enemy burst out of the Ardennes at 0530 on the morning of December 6, 1944. Amid the cold and snow of that frigid December morning came enemy tanks and foot soldiers camouflaged in white clothing and supported by some of Germany's finest. Major Otto Skorzeny and his 150th Panzer Brigade and Lieutenant Colonel Jochem Peiper's First SS Panzer Tank Unit led the attack. The rumors of a massive German troop build-up along the front turned out to be accurate and reinforced our confidence in the reports being received from the French underground. They had been constantly warning our high command to anticipate this "last ditch effort" by Hitler. The consequences of this action are well documented by World War II historians. The fiasco became a classic study of infantry and tank warfare. This was the infamous "Battle of the Bulge" in all its fury.
    While this onslaught took place between the German towns of Echternach in the south and Monchau in the north, our Division was occupied cleaning out strong points north and beyond Haguenau. Fighting the enemy, the bitter cold, pneumonia and the ever-present trench foot, we finally reached our objective, the town of Wissembourg on the French/German border, located along the Maginot Line. (The Maginot Line was made up of a long line of concrete bunkers intended to defend the French from German invasions.) Most of the civilians fled

One Soldier's Journey

when our troops approached. Those that remained displayed white sheets from their windows and rooftops indicating their surrender, hoping, of course, we would refrain from shelling their little village.

After we arrived at Wissembourg, which was around the middle of December 1944, we were able to rest, regroup and receive replacements for our killed and wounded. The amount of time that we spent there was the longest since we camped in Bayon after the disastrous skirmish at Foret de Parroy. We celebrated both Christmas and New Year's in Wissembourg and were privileged to have Captain (Father) Murphy, our regimental chaplain, visit our area. Father Murphy not only ministered to our non-Catholic soldiers, our Catholic soldiers had the rare opportunity to attend the celebration of Christmas Mass performed on the back bar of the town tavern amid the bottles of wine, liqueurs, schnapps and cognacs. After Mass, those bottles were quickly sorted out and "liberated" by our Company wine and liqueur connoisseurs.

As the Christmas season approached, the front lines became noticeably quiet. It became apparent that the German troops and our own soldiers had come to a common understanding about the upcoming holiday. While we huddled in our foxholes during the cold and frosty nights and at times while manning our outposts, strains of "O Tannenbaum" ("O Christmas Tree") or "Lili Marlene" could be heard off in the distance, coming from the German lines.

After a long absence of news from home, Christmas packages containing cookies, cakes, candies, plus letters began to be brought forward as long as the front lines remained still. On Christmas Day, we were even treated to a wonderful holiday dinner hand carried to the front lines by our wonderful and heroic kitchen personnel. Although the joy and magic of Christmas was everywhere, it was dampened many times by tears falling on love letters from home. The killing and maiming of men that we had been experiencing was shattering to the morale of the best soldiers, even more so at this time of the year. The constant question to me was, "Lieutenant, when will it be my turn?"

Because of this, I decided that it would be good for morale purposes if I could send two or three men at a time from each platoon back to the rear on a rotation schedule to enable them to rest and relax with our kitchen and supply personnel. This turned out to be an enormously popular program, never authorized by the upper command, but wonderful for morale. These men were now out of artillery and small arms range and, after two or three days of rest and relaxation, they could return to the front, rested and refreshed.

Psychologically perhaps, this was a self-serving exercise on my part because I was desperately trying to impress upon my men that I was a sincere, caring and concerned officer who truly appreciated their predicament. I also wanted them to assure their loved ones back home of my concern for their welfare. I really believe that goal was accomplished. I felt that their knowing I cared helped both them and their families to endure.

While we were situated in Wissembourg, we were attached to the 9th Army, commanded by General Bradley. We were placed on 100% alert, the intention being that we were to protect the southern flank of the "Bulge." We were extremely jumpy. Several days before the German attack at the Battle of the Bulge, Major Otto Skorzeny was reported to have dispatched about 500 German soldiers who had been instructed to infiltrate our lines. These soldiers were rumored to be dressed in American uniforms driving captured jeeps and wearing dog tags that had been removed from killed Americans. They spoke perfect English and most had been educated either in the United States or England. Their mission was to disrupt and confuse our troops with mis-information by changing road and street signs and by giving inaccurate directions to our MP traffic guides. Needless to say, we were all extremely suspicious of any strange face. We always challenged anyone who approached our encampment with the demand to respond with the correct password when confronted.

After the holidays, the skies began to clear. Our fighter planes, both P-47's and P-51's, were out in force much like a hive of enraged honey bees, strafing and bombing the retreating German troops while offering protection for our heavy bombers. (All of our heavy bombers that had been stationed in England were out in force and were re-establishing their heavy bombing runs.) From our position, we were able to faintly hear the thump, thump, thump of those massive aerial bombs as they were being dropped on German troops and major German cities. Mass, total destruction was their mission and in most instances it was accomplished. We were now all aware that the "Bulge" was contained and the enemy troops, in order to avoid being outflanked, were frantically retreating to the east.

The incessant bombing went on around the clock and the earth trembled as hundreds of bombers flew overhead. At night, the pyrotechnics of German ack-ack fire would illuminate the sky. Occasionally, one of the planes in our Flying Fortress Group or a British Lancaster would go down in flames. It was a

One Soldier's Journey

horrifying sight and my thoughts always were, "What happened to that brave crew?"

Chapter 29

Stalemate

Rittershoffen, France
Early to Mid-January 1945

Early in January 1945, in order to solidify the front and to comply with Eisenhower's and De Gaulle's agreement to defend a line from Saarbrücken, Germany, in the north to Strasbourg, France, in the south, we were transferred to the U.S. Seventh Army under Lieutenant General Alexander Patch. We were then quickly ordered south to establish a defensive perimeter around the town of Rittershoffen, a small semi-rural French city, which was located between Saarbrücken and Strasbourg.

As we marched into Rittershoffen, I had a strange, weird foreboding feeling. The streets were vacant. No men were seen anywhere and we suspected the women and children were all hiding in their cellars. There was a huge Catholic church situated close to the town square, just outside our intended defensive perimeter. When our troops entered the town, the bell in that church began to toll, slow and measured, not unlike a funeral dirge. (It would later be rung in homage to our many fallen brave soldiers.)

Putting aside my feelings of impending danger for the moment, and with the help of Lieutenants Perkins and Shelton, I quickly established a defensive perimeter around the city. We placed automatic weapons in the hands of each platoon member stationed along the perimeter and coordinated our activities with I and K Companies on our right and left flanks. M Company set up an observer to direct 81mm mortar fire to our front if needed. We then established

One Soldier's Journey

communications with each platoon leader using field telephones and radios. (Radios were placed in the field in case our telephone wires were cut by enemy artillery, which happened frequently.) Then, after I plotted-in defensive artillery coordinates on our frontlines, I felt that no one on God's green earth could possibly breach our perimeter. We were no longer foxhole soldiers but were concealed and placed behind fences, stone cattle barns and stone and stucco houses. Our BAR (Browning Automatic Rifles) machine guns and mortars were hidden, camouflaged by haystacks and manure piles.

Unknown to us at the time when we moved our defensive line south from Wissembourg to Rittershoffen, Germany's Oberst (Colonel) Hans von Luck's 125th Regiment of the 21st Panzer Division followed us into Wissembourg. There he was given the mission to break through the Maginot[16] Line at Rittershoffen. We were totally unaware of this plan. (Von Luck became a German Colonel at the age of thirty-three. He was a brilliant German officer who proudly possessed the Knight's Cross.)

Colonel von Luck had earlier committed his 124th Panzergrenadier Regiment against our Normandy landing on Juno and Sword beaches. His regiment's mission was to defend the French City of Caen against the 50th British Division and the Canadian 3rd Division but he had been absent on a three-day leave. When he returned, his deputy told him that there was nothing left of his battle group with which to fight.

Fortunately, after our troops were in place around Rittershoffen, we had plenty of time to improve and fortify our defensive positions, clean and oil our weapons, and hoard and inventory our ammunition. We even had time to send "thank-you" notes back home for all the Christmas gifts and goodies that we had received from family and friends. Also, our Second Battalion had established another defensive perimeter around the town of Hatten, located approximately five kilometers north of us. The 14th Armored Division supported both of their flanks with strategically placed Sherman M-1 tanks to help defend our position there. As might be expected, these tanks became prime targets for von Luck's Tiger tanks and their deadly 88's. Thus, the stage was set for one of the fiercest battles of World War II.

I first became aware of Colonel von Luck's impending attack upon our position on January 9, 1945, around 0400 hours. It was a bitter cold and frosty

---

[16] A line of defensive fortifications built before World War II to protect the eastern border of France

night. Steam was rising from our GI-issued canteen cups of boiling coffee heated on makeshift stoves and over open hearths of abandoned farmhouses. The first indication of trouble was our sighting of tracer bullets being fired over our heads coming from the direction of the enemy lines. I knew at once that this was it. The Germans always used this tactic to guide their troops in the right direction, especially at night. Next came the clanking and rumbling of German tanks, accompanied again by infantry cloaked in white sheets that made them almost invisible against the January blanket of snow on the ground.

About the same time that the Germans were announcing their arrival with their directional tracer bullets, there was an enormous explosion on my right flank, which erupted into a fireball of exploding heavy-caliber ammunition. Instantly, I had the sickening realization that one of our tanks was lost and destroyed. Then, through the haze, fog and smoke of battle appeared a lone, surviving tank crew member running toward my command bunker in a state of shock and panic, blood streaming down and across his eyes. One of my Company's medics and I stopped him and were horrified to see the shocking sight of three-fourths of his scalp torn away, detached from his skull, laying across his forehead. Gently and calmly the young medical corporal replaced the torn scalp, stopped the bleeding, securely bandaged his head and assisted him to our Battalion Aid Station for further medical help. Through the grapevine, I later heard that the wound had healed and, although several hundred stitches were required to mend his gaping wound, his scars were unnoticeable, covered by the hair on his head. *(This was just one of many examples of heroism by our Army medics who came to be affectionately called "Doc" throughout the war.)*

Even though our MLR was waiting for them, the initial German assault against our lines was brutal and deadly. There was much hand-to-hand and grisly bayonet fighting and when their tanks eventually moved in, we had to withdraw about 200 yards back and establish a new line of defense.

Rittershoffen eventually became a stalemate. We held most of the town to our rear. Across the street, the enemy shouted obscenities at us in German. Our GI's responded with the nastiest names they could muster-up. "Up your wiener schnitzel, Schweinhund!" When the Germans heard that, I'm sure they thought that those American GI's were really a tough bunch of hombres!

Much to our disadvantage, the Germans captured that huge Catholic church across the street from where our troops were positioned and used it like

One Soldier's Journey

an early Roman fortress. From the church steeple, they could observe our every move. Consequently, any troop deployment, replenishment of rations and ammunition plus the evacuation of our dead and wounded were done at night. This situation became extremely perplexing for our troops and totally unacceptable to our battalion commander.

Eventually, I received a radio order from battalion headquarters. "Thome, I want you to send one of your platoons across the street and capture that damn church!" I tried to explain to Colonel Eason that it would be impossible to comply with that order since neither the Germans nor our troops could enter that street without being cut to ribbons.

Eason remained absolutely adamant. "Damn it, Thome, that church must be taken and neutralized at all costs!" I discussed the situation with Lieutenants Perkins and Shelton, and we all agreed that it would be suicide to attempt such an outrageous mission. We came up with a plan. We decided that our front line, upon my signal, would simultaneously fire all of their weapons - machine guns, mortars, bazookas, rifles and hand grenades. I then gave my command to fire. The resulting noise from our demonstration of small arms fire was deafening and could be heard for miles around.

After about five or six minutes of this, I radioed back to my commander and told him that we were pinned down and had to withdraw. His response was, "Thome, you and your men are doing one hell of a job up there. We could hear all of that action back here and I want you to know how much I appreciate your efforts." Little did he know that we never left our positions. He was far to the rear, deep in his bunker as usual, and I knew it. My troops were grateful to me for employing such a deceitful plan because I had again demonstrated that I would never expose them to any damn fool dangerous mission if it could possibly be avoided.

Earlier during the German pre-dawn attack on our defensive perimeter, I experienced a moment of sheer panic. The shoulder strap on my gas mask that was attached to my combat uniform became entangled in a barbed wire fence and forced me to stop dead in my tracks, exposed to the enemy. I had been working my way along our front lines, shouting words of encouragement to my men. All of a sudden, it seemed as if every German shell had my name on it. They were exploding and pummeling the ground all around me. It appeared as if I would never be able to free myself. Escape seemed impossible. I figured I was a dead man. Frantically, I reached for my trench knife and cut the strap that held me prisoner, left my gas mask hanging on the fence, and dove for cover. Much to the credit of the Germans and the Allies, poison gas was never used during the war, although there were times when we were put on the alert and gas masks were hastily distributed.

Because of our determined resistance to Colonel von Luck's offensive, he called the 25th Grenadier Division and an entire regiment of Germany's crack 7th Parachute Division into the fray. We retaliated by adding small units of the Negro 827th Tank Destroyer Battalion plus tank men and armored infantry from our 14th Armored Division. Those young Negro soldiers were fearless. They protected us from German flame-throwing tanks that continually assaulted our machine gun strong points, and they destroyed several German Tiger tanks through their courageous actions. Those of us whose lives they saved will always remember them.[17]

---

[17] The United States armed forces were not integrated during World War II. After years of study and foot dragging by the armed services and others, in 1948, President Harry Truman issued Executive Order #9981 ordering them to stop segregation. It took several years to achieve.

Chapter 30

Lieutenant Kilev

Battle of Rittershoffen, France
January 19, 1945

    Our Second Battalion had established a perimeter around Hatten to the north of us and was now cut off and surrounded by the enemy. Since we were unable to keep them supplied in the usual manner, blood plasma, supplies and rations were stuffed into empty 155mm artillery shells and then literally shot over to them. Several airdrops were also attempted, but our supplies and rations only fell into enemy hands. Three companies with their dead and wounded were isolated in Hatten for a total of 48 hours before counter attacking American troops could rescue them.

    Back in Rittershoffen, due to the dark winter nights and the continual probing by German patrols, we found it necessary to continually shoot up flares in order to illuminate the countryside, which would hopefully deter sneak attacks under the cloak of darkness. When our flare supply was exhausted, we would pick out a building or house in the enemy sector, and radio the map coordinates to our artillery people who would then immediately dispatch a 155mm white phosphorous incendiary shell that would ignite the building and light up the area until daylight. Every night we would choose a different building. We all figured that this outraged the Germans because we knew those burned out houses were being used by them for shelter.

    Time, *Newsweek* and *The New York Times* all attempted to describe the battle at Hatten and Rittershoffen but Stephen E. Ambrose described it best in

One Soldier's Journey

his *Citizen Soldiers*. Ambrose stated that von Luck, "a veteran of Poland, France, Russia, North Africa and Normandy," characterized this battle as "one of the hardest and most costly battles ever raged." Both sides used artillery non-stop, firing 10,000 rounds a day. Both the Germans and the Allies suffered terrible losses and many innocent civilians became tragic victims of this crazy brutality. Stephen Ambrose stated in *Citizen Soldiers* that the Seventh Army's casualties, which included our battalion, were 11,609 plus 2,836 cases of trench foot. Germany's losses were around 23,000 killed, wounded or missing and the Seventh Army processed some 5,986 POWs (Prisoners of War). He mentioned that some 100 civilians lay dead in the streets. I only know that I lost about 35-40 men, either wounded or killed. I do not know how I survived.

On the morning of January 19, 1945, as the ebb and flow of battle continued, from my position between our two front line platoons, I heard a clanking and rumbling that sounded very much like the approach of one of our M1 tanks. As I looked around, I could hardly believe my eyes. Right down the main street of Rittershoffen and heading right toward that damnable Catholic church near the town square came an M-1 Tank with a self-propelled 250mm cannon. It seemed to be the size of a freight train and was just a little noisier. Lieutenant Ed Kilev was in the driver's seat and he had that cannon pointed directly at the church steeple. As he approached the target, he was partially protected by the protective shield on the gun mount. The enemy fire he attracted was enormous. With a gigantic blast from the muzzle of the tank's cannon, a huge portion of the church was pulverized.

Lieutenant Kilev then retreated and drove away. To our amazement, he reappeared the next morning, drove within 100 yards of the church and blasted it again. The church steeple finally disappeared in a cloud of dust and rubble. You can imagine our jubilation!

Ed Kilev's courage in taking out that church and church steeple, a strategic enemy stronghold, in the midst of relentless enemy artillery fire, was the most heroic act I ever witnessed while fighting the enemy. For his actions he was awarded the Silver Star.

One Soldier's Journey

AWARD OF SILVER STAR

Pursuant to authority contained in AR600-45, the Silver Star is awarded to the following officer. First Lieutenant EDWARD V. KILEV, 01177127. 575 Field Artillery Battalion, United States Army, for gallantry in action against the enemy on 19 January 1945 in France.

IN THE FACE OF INTENSE ENEMY FIRE, LIEUTENANT KILEV MANEUVERED HIS SELF-PROPELLED CANNON IN A POSITION WITHIN 200 YARDS OF AN ENEMY OBSERVATION

POST AND STRONGPOINT, PLACED DIRECT FIRE AT THE POSITION AND DENIED THE ENEMY OBSERVATION OF FRIENDLY INSTALLATIONS. UPON COMPLETION OF HIS MISSION HE WITHDREW HIS WEAPON, RETURNING THE NEXT DAY TO FIRE FROM A POSITION LESS THAN A 100 YARDS AWAY FROM THE ENEMY EMPLACEMENT. THE COURAGE DISPLAYED BY LIEUTENANT KILEV REFLECTS HIGH CREDIT ON HIMSELF AND THE ARMED FORCES OF THE UNITED STATES. ENTERED MILITARY SERVICE FROM THE DISTRICT OF COLUMBIA.

An interesting note relative to the battle of Rittershoffen was that on the first day of battle, during all of the chaos and confusion, I received word from our battalion commander that we had just acquired another replacement captain. He was to be assigned to my Company L. Again, I was to be second in command or Executive Officer. I waited to turn over my company to the new captain, but he never arrived. Somewhere along the trail from the Officer Replacement Depot to the front, our new captain apparently became sidetracked, perhaps in Luneville or Nancy, and contracted a severe case of gonorrhea. He was immediately evacuated for medical treatment, and I never saw or heard from him again. When they were told, many of the Company L soldiers exclaimed, "Great! Better than a million-dollar wound!"

One Soldier's Journey

For service to my country during the horrific battle to safeguard the city of Rittershoffen and the village of Hatten from the enemy, a battle in which I never expected to survive, I was awarded a Bronze Star Oak-Leaf Cluster.[18]

AWARD OF BRONZE STAR OAK-LEAF CLUSTER

Pursuant to authority contained in AR600-45, in addition to the Bronze Star Medal previously awarded, a Bronze Star Oak-Leaf Cluster is awarded to the following officer,

First Lieutenant JAMES L. THOME, 01313514, Infantry, 315 Infantry Regiment, United States Army, for meritorious achievement in action against the enemy from January 11, 1945 to 20 January 1945 in France

DURING THE ENGAGEMENT IN RITTERSHOFFEN, 11 TO 20 JANUARY 1945, LT. THOME PERFORMED ALL MISSIONS ASSIGNED TO HIM IN AN EXEMPLARY MANNER. FOR THE FIRST FEW DAYS OF THE ENGAGEMENT, LT. THOME ACTED AS COMPANY EXECUTIVE OFFICER AND WHEN TWO PLATOON LEADERS BECAME CASUALTIES, HE TOOK COMMAND OF BOTH THE FIRST AND SECOND PLATOONS AND LED THEM THROUGHOUT THE REMAINDER OF THE ENGAGEMENT IN A MANNER THAT DISTINGUISHED HIM AS ONE OF THE OUTSTANDING OFFICERS IN HIS BATTALION. MANY TIMES HE EXPOSED HIMSELF TO HEAVY ENEMY FIRE TO DIRECT HIS MEN IN THE ATTACK. LT. THOME'S SUPERIOR DEVOTION TO DUTY REFLECTS HIGHEST CREDIT TO HIMSELF AND TO HIS ORGANIZATION. SIGNED: ROGER S. RYAN, CAPTAIN, INF. APPROVED: ANDREW J. SCHRIVER, JR., COLONEL, INF.

---

[18] An "oak-leaf cluster" denotes a second or succeeding award of a medal, in this case, the Bronze Star.

Chapter 31

Private Bill Newman Missing!

Tongres, Belgium
February 1945

Finally, on January 20, 1944, Hatten and Rittershoffen were successfully evacuated and we established new positions on the Moder River. The enemy was very slow to follow up on this move and it wasn't until the night of January 24 that the Germans attempted to assault our new lines. Their parachute, Panzer grenadier and their SS Panzer divisions, the same units we fought in Rittershoffen, secured bridgeheads on the south bank of the river but at an extremely costly price. The number of enemy dead and wounded ran high and our division's prisoner of war cage was filled many times over. The next day the Germans called it quits and pulled back north of the river. On 17 February our crippled and battered 79th Division was relieved of its position by the 36th and 101st Divisions and we assembled at Pont-a-Mousson on the Moder River for a much-needed rest.

It wasn't until the following July that the War Department finally recognized our unbelievable efforts in the defense of Rittershoffen and issued War Department General Orders Number 54, 12 July 1945.

For its inspired defense against overwhelming enemy forces at Rittershoffen last January, in which it played a large part in preventing what may have been a major German breakthrough in Alsace, the third Battalion has

been awarded **PRESIDENTIAL CITATION. Commanded by Lt. Col. Thomas K. Eason, the Battalion is the third within the Regiment to win this high honor.**

THE 3RD BATTALION, 315TH INFANTRY REGIMENT, IS CITED FOR EXTRAORDINARY GALLANTRY, INDOMITABLE COURAGE, TENACITY OF PURPOSE AND HIGH ESPRIT DE CORPS DISPLAYED IN THE ACCOMPLISHMENT OF UNUSUALLY DIFFICULT COMBAT OPERATION AGAINST THE ENEMY DURING THE PERIOD OF 9 JANUARY 1945 TO 20 JANUARY 1945 IN THE VICINITY OF RITTERSHOFFEN, ALSACE, FRANCE. WHEN ENEMY FORCES HAD EFFECTED A PENETRATION THROUGH FRIENDLY LINES AND A BREAKTHROUGH APPEARED IMMINENT, THE 3RD BATTALION, 315TH REGIMENT, WAS COMMITTED TO HALT THE ENEMY ONSLAUGHT. ALTHOUGH CONFRONTED BY THE ELITE OF THE ENEMY'S FORCES, THIS INSPIRED BATTALION REPULSED REPEATED FANATICAL, TANK-INFANTRY ATTACKS INFLICTING SEVERE LOSSES ON NUMERICALLY SUPERIOR ATTACKERS, DESPITE THE HANDICAP OF SHORTAGES IN CERTAIN TYPES OF AMMUNITION AND EQUIPMENT. THE SHEER COURAGE AND INVINCIBLE WILL DISPLAYED BY THE 3RD BATTALION. 315TH REGIMENT, IS IN KEEPING WITH THE HIGHEST TRADITIONS OF THE AMERICAN INFANTRY AND REFLECTS GREAT CREDIT ON THE ARMED FORCES OF THE UNITED STATES.

I was there, and the Presidential Citation says it all. It was noted and signed by President Franklin D. Roosevelt. It was an extremely high honor.

After a brief interlude at our rest area in Pont-a-Mousson, we were again placed on alert to prepare to move out. Our hot meals, hot showers and change of clean clothes abruptly ended. It became apparent that our rest period was now over and again we were on the chase and off to battle.

One Soldier's Journey

On 14 February 1945, the 79th Division was alerted to prepare for rail and motor movement northward in order to join up with the Ninth Army and XVI Corps. Five days later, we were situated in the vicinity of Tongres, Belgium. We soon discovered that this move had been ordered so that the 79th Division could be set-up and positioned in such a way that when the time came, we could lead an assault across the Rhine River. It also dawned on us that whenever we did an outstanding job, the demands on our division never seemed to stop. They only appeared to increase. The 79th Division had the reputation of being an outstanding combat unit. As a result, impossible missions never ceased being assigned to us.

The components of the 79th Division consisted of three Regiments, namely the 313th, the 314th and the 315th along with artillery units comprised of 105mm and 155mm howitzer battalions, medics, MPs, motor pool technicians, supply and other service units. I was assigned to the 315th Regiment, which consisted of three battalions.

The First Battalion consisted of Companies A, B, C & D. The Second Battalion included Companies E, F, G & H. Companies I, K, L & M made up the Third Battalion. Of all these companies that made up the 315th Regiment, I could never understand why my Company L was always selected to be one of the lead companies in an attack, especially since Company L was the reserve company in my battalion. Also, my battalion was the reserve battalion in the regiment and my Regiment was the reserve regiment in my division. When I learned that we were ordered to prepare to cross over the Rhine River to capture the east bank and then move on to Berlin, I was almost certain that Company L would lead the way. How right I was.

After camp had been set up outside of Tongres, I organized a minimum perimeter defense line in and around my area of responsibility. While I waited further orders, Lieutenant Bart Walker and I decided that we ought to take a jeep and sneak back to Liege, which was located about nine kilometers south and west of our camp. Tongres, at this time, was considered safe and neutralized except for a few diehard Nazi snipers, whom we promptly dispatched. This was also the case in Liege. The war had by-passed this large Belgian city and it was again thriving with theaters, bistros and nightlife.

When we entered the city, we found it to be teeming with rear echelon army personnel - medics, nurses, quartermaster corps, transportation corps and communication people, along with the Air Force support groups, most in their

Class A uniforms. We stopped at an MP Station on the outskirts of town to find out "where the action was." While looking us over in our steel helmets, battle fatigue clothing, and cartridge belts with our 45 caliber "grease" gun automatic weapons slung over our shoulders, I am certain the MP on duty would have loved to chase us out of town. We were perhaps the first combat soldiers he had met and he probably wasn't too sure what our reaction would be, so he finally directed us to a local theater, which contained a large ballroom in its basement where weekly dances were held.

An Army orchestra was playing all the Glen Miller wartime melodies and the Red Cross volunteers were dancing with the rear echelon dandies when Bart and I walked in. A hush fell over the room and it appeared that contempt and disdain were directed toward us much like a couple of western outlaws arriving in an old time saloon. On every face in the room was a look of, "How dare you!" It appeared to us that we might be in the wrong place. Nevertheless, we hung our burp guns across the back of our chairs, ordered a bottle of red wine and settled back to enjoy the music while looking tough and menacing to all the rear echelon twinkle-toes with their clean shaven faces and polished boots.

Suddenly, Bart appeared to be extremely startled and called my attention to a second lieutenant who was dancing with an army nurse. He exclaimed that the lieutenant on the dance floor was one of our machine gunners (an enlisted man) who was supposed to have been killed by a German flame-throwing tank back in Rittershoffen. How could this be that he was now back in Liege in an officer's uniform, dancing and having a good time? We both jumped up simultaneously and proceeded across the dance floor to confront him. He saw us coming and quickly disappeared into the crowd.

Bart and I both acknowledged to one another that the men who were killed in Rittershoffen were so badly burned that unless dog tags were found on their bodies, identification was next to impossible. At Rittershoffen, we had reported Bill Newman as KIA. He was in a machine gun squad there and now appeared to be the lieutenant we discovered on the dance floor in Liege. Did Bill Newman switch dog tags, and was he actually alive, impersonating an officer?

Approximately two years after my Army service was terminated; I received a letter from the Graves Registration Department, Quartermaster Corps, requesting information on the circumstances of William Newman's death and perhaps the location of his burial site. Apparently, Newman's parents were

One Soldier's Journey
planning a trip to France to visit his gravesite but the Army couldn't locate it. All the memories of that night on the dance floor in Liege returned and I told my story to the Quartermasters Corps. I never heard from them again. After fifty plus years, I've often wondered whether Bill Newman is still alive, somewhere in Europe and, if so, does he miss his relatives and loved ones.

Chapter 32

Operation Flashpoint

Brunssum, Holland
March 1945

There seemed to be an atmosphere of guarded peace and tranquillity surrounding us during our respite on the Belgian and Dutch borders. It began to appear that our unrelenting pursuit of the enemy was finally overcoming their fanatical resistance. The prisoners we had been capturing were mostly older men from the German Volksturm units and younger boys in their teens. Most were eager and anxious to surrender rather than face our devastating artillery, small arms fire and perhaps the wrath of the Russians who were closing in on the eastern front.

On the busy dusty roads near our front line perimeter, streams of two-wheeled pushcarts were being guided along by the very elderly, all loaded with household possessions they had saved when they were routed from their homes. A grandmother and perhaps a younger woman trailed by two or three little children in ragged clothing and worn out shoes usually accompanied them. A few younger men were also observed dressed in civilian clothes, also ragged and torn. We all knew that they were deserters from the German army who had shed their uniforms. Many were foreign ex-slave laborers, deserters from Nazi work gangs who had finally discovered freedom. Many of my men shared their rations with these poor and destitute refugees, most especially with the little children whose innocence brought lumps to our throats. All the people that we saw were friendly, enthusiastic and extremely happy to see us, soldiers from America.

One Soldier's Journey

The civilians who were passing through our lines to the rear were most anxious to discover how their little farms, homes and cattle survived the ravishes of war. Upon their arrival, most experienced total hopelessness. Their homes, barns and little villages, by most accounts, lay in ruin, totally destroyed, as were their cattle, horses and other livestock that lay bloated and rotting in the bomb-cratered fields. Many explored the areas for fresh dug burial sites because those civilians who were killed in the onslaught were usually temporarily buried where they died.

In spite of the streams of refugees returning to their homes through our lines, our assault to the south continued with all its fury. Our Air Force literally flew unchallenged and continued to bomb the highly occupied industrial Ruhr Valley in Germany with mammoth explosives and fire bombs. The German army was retreating east of the Rhine River and had gathered in what was later called the Ruhr Pocket. This was an enclave that contained thousands of SS troops and other die-hard Nazi soldiers who had retreated to this area. Our task now became apparent. We had to protect the north flank to prevent a breakout from their encirclement. We had to cross the Rhine into Germany in order to surround the Germans in the Essen area and to neutralize them from further fighting. My Company L was chosen to participate, just as I had earlier predicted.

Late on a cold and blustery March evening, we received an order to prepare immediately to move north to the Netherlands-German border town of Brunssum, Holland. It was here that we were to prepare for "Operation Flashpoint." This was the code word for the crossing of the Rhine River. Brunssum was within a few kilometers of the Maas River, which closely resembled the Rhine in width, rate of flow and depth. It was there we trained for two weeks in river crossing operations.

The crossing of the Rhine was to be planned and controlled by navy personnel. They were to supply us with boats that would be equipped to carry nine men, two navy crewmen and seven army infantrymen. They would be outfitted with fifty-five horse-powered motors to propel them swiftly across the river. Each seven-man team of infantrymen would hand-carry, in addition to his personal equipment, a maximum amount of rations, ammunition and medical supplies. These supplies would be dumped on the far side of the river because we all knew that it would take a considerable period of time before a pontoon bridge could be installed for supplies to reach us.

One Soldier's Journey

A quartering party preceded us to Brunssum and arranged to have each Holland home furnish shelter for one, two or three GI's. The townspeople were most accommodating, friendly and cordial toward the Americans. Some of our men slept in cellars, some in barns and several were even furnished spare bedrooms. I set up my command post and communications people in the Wollersheim family home at 17 Limbergerweg. Mama Wollersheim was a widow whose husband was killed in a coal mine accident. I knew that she could certainly use the stipend that the Army would pay her for the use of her home.

Sergeant John Walker, our mess sergeant, set up his mess quarters in Mama Wollersheim's kitchen and our chow line was in her back yard. Before I became aware of it, I believe we were feeding most of the little neighborhood children who began to appear in our chow line along with our soldiers. Sergeant Walker even started to keep a roster of the neighborhood wives who took turns picking up our used coffee grounds. Coffee was such a luxury in an area where the Germans confiscated everything. The Wollersheims, like most of the Dutch in that vicinity, were of average financial means but there was nothing available to buy. Simple things, ordinary staples like flour, coffee, tea, shortening and sugar were impossible to come by, as was all description of clothing. Absolutely nothing was available. The Germans had taken it all when they retreated.

Mia, one of the Wollersheim children who lived at home was pregnant. Her husband, Pete, was in the Dutch army, which was currently being reorganized clandestinely. Mia and the entire town were convinced that when we attempted to cross the Rhine in our small boats, we would all be blown out of the water and killed. I told Mia, "Nonsense, Mia, we will cross the Rhine and the war will be over. I'll return to America and send you and Pete a complete layette for that little baby in your belly."

All the neighbors scoffed at my promise and said that we wouldn't have a chance crossing the Rhine and even if we did, I would soon forget Brunssum when I returned to America. A few months later, and after VE[19] Day, when I was back home, I sent Pete and Mia a package. The entire town turned out to watch them as they unpacked a marvelous assortment of baby gifts including a

---

[19] Victory in Europe.

One Soldier's Journey

complete layette, a thoroughly unexpected surprise from America. I kept my promise to those wonderful and unselfish people I had come to respect and love.

Chapter 33

Our Turn

Brunssum, Holland
March 23, 1945

During our two weeks of intensive training in Brunssum, I was angered at hearing of the barbaric behavior of the German troops while they had occupied this quaint Dutch town. Not only did they confiscate everything they could carry off that wasn't nailed down, bicycles included, they also stripped wedding bands right off the fingers of married women they caught on the streets, along with any other jewelry found worn on their person. Consequently, the women refused to wear their wedding rings and other precious jewelry in public. This created somewhat of a minor dilemma among our more amorous GI's. "Geeze, Lieutenant, aren't any of the women married in this town?" was a common question.

Many very warm relationships developed among our soldiers and the residents of Brunssum during our stay as their uninvited guests. Despite the comfortable feelings generated by such close camaraderie, we were still all very aware of the difficult and dangerous mission that lay ahead.

On the afternoon of March 11, 1945, Colonel Eason informed me that out of our entire regiment and battalion my Company L along with Company K were selected to be the two leading assault teams to cross the Rhine River. He also informed me, since I was one of the company commanders to lead the assault across the Rhine, I could have the opportunity to report back to a grassy landing field in our rear area where an L-5 Piper Cub artillery observation plane would be

One Soldier's Journey

made available to me. I could use it to reconnoiter my zone of attack on the other side of the river. I jumped at the chance, inasmuch as our crossing would be made before sunrise and I was afraid there would be considerable confusion in the dark.

As I was flown near the opposite shore, I observed many German troops fortifying their dug-in gun emplacements in front of our sector. I imagined that when our assault boats started their engines, German flares would illuminate the sky and we would become excellent targets for the enemy. My thoughts were suddenly interrupted when our plane became the recipient of a rapid burst of enemy machine gun fire. The radio, which was mounted above and directly in back of me, was shattered and a hail of broken radio tubes and parts rained down on my head and neck. I quickly patted the pilot, who was seated in front of me, on the shoulder and alerted him about the damaged radio. He smiled, gave me a "thumbs up" signal, quickly made a big U-turn (a "180") and headed straight back to the safety of our landing strip. Throughout the next two weeks, those German fortifications that I had observed from the air remained a bothersome worry for me.

The plan to storm across the Rhine River was probably the best-prepared exercise in military history. The schedules of events as they were to occur were made months in advance. The magnitude of preparedness was unprecedented. As *Time* magazine reported in its April 2, 1945, issue, "Night and day along every road rolled tanks, guns and endless truck convoys carrying every conceivable weapon of destruction. In one area, ammunition was piled high for nearly twenty miles on each side of the highway. Every farm was an arsenal, every meadow and woodland concealed equipment and troops. The greatest smoke screen ever used in warfare stretched sixty-six miles from Nijmegen to Dusseldorf. Daily sorties from the Eighth Air Force averaged from 4,000 to 8,000 tons [of bombs] and finally reached 12,000 tons, 1,000 more than D-Day."

Our crossing was also supported by artillery parked almost hub to hub stretching for miles both north and south from our area. The roar and blast of constant cannon fire prior to our assault contributed to several cases of severe combat fatigue (shell shock) within my company as we began our approach to the shore. I had to evacuate these men as quickly as possible before it became contagious. On our side of the Rhine, more than 1,100 big guns sent barrage after barrage of unparalleled proportion hurling through the smoke screen. In addition to this, the Allied First Airborne was to make a drop immediately to our front to prevent the Germans from counter attacking our landing. With all of this firepower and airborne support to back us up, I had the utmost confidence that our crossing would be a complete success.

Our division was under the command of the Ninth Army's General Simpson. The British Second and the Canadian First Division under General Montgomery supported us. From their bases in England, heavy bombers hammered the Ruhr Valley day and night.

As we continued to prepare for the crossing, the Germans were unable to gauge its magnitude on our side of the Rhine since smoke pots obscured their view.

On March 22, 1945, at 0100 hours, our motorized column left Brunssum en route to our line of departure on the banks of the Rhine. Just about the entire town of Brunssum turned out in the darkness to bid us good-bye and wish me and my Company L, "God speed." Mama Wollersheim and her family shook my hand and wished me a tearful good-bye while I assured Mia to anticipate her baby's gifts arriving in the near future. She had a doubtful look in her eyes but I was convinced that she really did believe that I would survive, somehow.

The great assault began on March 23. At 1900 hours our Allied troops began to cross the Rhine in sequence. The British 51st Highland Division in the north under Montgomery was first. At 2000 hours, a brigade of British commandos crossed and waited 1,500 yards from Wesel until a thunderous fleet of bombers pounded the city. The British then charged into the city and with their bayonets and grenades rooted out the shocked Germans. It was now 2200 hours. It was our turn.

General Patton had just stood on a pontoon bridge south of us and urinated in the river while admonishing the Germans with, "Here's to you, you Nazi sons-of-bitches and your Rhine River!"

As we approached our boats on the riverbank, each soldier was handed an inflatable life preserver, which was activated by a gas cartridge, to wear around his waist. I quickly entered my assigned boat, inserted my gas cartridge and discovered that in spite of all the planning, my cartridge turned out to be a dud. "My God, I didn't want to drown in the Rhine River!" The section of the river where we were to cross was anywhere from four to six feet in depth and approximately 200 to 300 yards wide. It was imperative that everyone wear inflatable life vests so that no one would drown if a boat were to be blasted out

One Soldier's Journey

of the water by direct artillery fire from the Germans on the opposite side of the river. We were assembled alongside the banks of the Rhine ready to go, and there I stood with a defective life preserver cartridge in my sweaty hand!

Chapter 34

On to Berlin!

Essen, Germany
Early April 1945

    The preening and posturing of some of our military commanders always fascinated me. Most of them were terribly egocentric and highly competitive, and they seemed to attempt to elevate their importance by displaying a particular affectation that would eventually become known as their personal signature. Whether it was Monty's ridiculous mustache, tam and riding crop; Churchill's "V" sign; MacArthur's corn cob pipe and his crushed Air Corps visor cap; Roosevelt's ubiquitous cigarette holder; or Patton's ever present ivory-handled pistols, they all insisted on having their own personal trademark. Not surprisingly, Patton always insisted that Eisenhower invented the shortened Eisenhower jacket so that his staff could kiss his ass.

    So there we were on the banks of the Rhine River; poised to embark on our mission to cross over and rout the Germans, while upstream stood Churchill, Monty and General Simpson all wishing us dogfaces God speed, waiting for *The Stars and Stripes* newspaper photographers to arrive. They all wanted to have their pictures taken "up front," thinking that this would be a wonderful morale builder for the folks back home. I really thought that is what they believed.

    We were finally given the command to move out from the riverbank in our assault boats. Much to our surprise, as we made our way across the Rhine, the Germans did not fire any flares over the river and we did not encounter any enemy artillery fire or small arms fire from the bank on the other side. It took us

One Soldier's Journey

about twenty minutes to cross and disembark. (I thought of George Washington crossing the Delaware River sans icebergs.) It appeared that our river crossing was going to be unopposed. As we came ashore and moved forward, we stepped very lightly in fear that the riverbank was highly salted with anti-personnel mines ready to detonate at the slightest jarring of the ground along our path. Nothing!

Our first phase line was to capture and control an elevated railroad track close to our point of landing. Located behind it was a heavily fortified German bunker, a gun position that I had spotted on my previous aerial reconnaissance flight over the area. I slowly crept up to it and positioned myself as close as I could, removed a grenade hanging from my cartridge belt, pulled its pin and lobbed it over the train tracks and into the bunker. There it exploded into an empty German dugout. A miracle! The enemy had completely evacuated their Rhine defenses and we walked in unscathed.

The Army and the Corps commanders were absolutely amazed at our good fortune and we quickly took advantage of it. We immediately began our build-up by utilizing all available Army and Navy watercraft to ferry men and equipment across the Rhine. By evening after a bitter fight, the city of Dinslaken had been captured. The 79th Division had now gained a large foothold on the East bank of the Rhine River.

How did we manage to have such good luck? Perhaps the Germans were forced to pull all of their troops back except for a few outposts along the river and hold their main forces in the rear for a possible counter attack. We had heard they were experiencing a desperate manpower crisis. Perhaps it was the great expanse of our military assault, our overwhelming air and artillery effort and the speed in which our troops poured across the river. Whatever the reason, our offensive tactic now became very clear. On to Berlin!

After regrouping in Dinslaken, our Division swung south and drove for the Rhine-Herne Kanal. On March 30, the canal was reached after we had overrun countless German towns along the way, which included Bottrop, Gladback and Oberhausen. We were now poised on the outskirts of Essen that, according to intelligence reports, was being heavily defended by crack German SS Troops. It was here we paused while attack plans were formulated.

Monumental efforts were being made to effect a plan for the invasion and capture of Essen from the Germans. The plan included a support drop of airborne paratroopers along with an attack from three different directions by three Army infantry divisions. While Corps Command Headquarters was embroiled in final strategy sessions, my company was deployed south of Essen. Our main mission was to prevent German entry through our assigned area of defense, which was a bridge leading into the city. We were told to defend that bridge at all costs. We set up a heavily guarded roadblock across the bridge, and I was assigned a tank destroyer to help me maintain our position.

Late in the afternoon, a young NCO from an anti-tank unit reported to me and asked where I would like to have the destroyer positioned. I pointed out the location to him. He informed me that his unit was assembled about a kilometer to our rear and that he would return within an hour with the destroyer. With that, he saluted, jumped into his jeep and left. About three hours later, I received an urgent radio message ordering me to immediately report to Division Headquarters for a high level conference. When I arrived, I discovered that when the young tanker left me in his jeep, he became lost and confused and wound up in the center of Essen, which was unbelievably undefended by the Germans. The generals, the colonels and intelligence people were shocked. So again, everything changed.

It was decided that "Lieutenant Thome will take Company L, and in a column of two's will march through the center of Essen." As we wound our way through the rubble, destruction and chaos of the city, white sheets appeared from windows signaling surrender. Old men in civilian clothes began to appear from blasted out buildings. The destruction of the city was horrible. As my company proceeded along the littered streets, I had the opportunity to climb atop a bombed out building that was about two stories high. As I looked around in all directions, there was not a taller structure in sight. Everything that had been standing had been flattened.

As we continued to proceed through the city, a young mother ran out from a rubble strewn building holding a little three-year-old girl in her arms. Both her legs had been amputated mid calf. As she held her daughter out to me she said, "Please take her to America. Show them what your bombs have done. They will take care of her better over there." What could I do? What could I say? I reached in my backpack and handed her a couple of K rations.

Chapter 35

Displaced Prisoners

Bochum and Mulheim, Germany
Mid-April 1945

Hitler's Third Reich was crumbling. More and more civilian men began to emerge from the ruins of Essen and all of them were quick to avow, "Nicht Nazi." I wondered where in the hell all those German bastards had gone.

Our entire Division continued east out of Essen and we were most anxious to exploit any opportunity to further rout and destroy the enemy. My Company L was at the head of a unit of a long column of troops leading the way, followed by soldiers from battalion, regiment and division that included elements from quartermasters, communications, artillery and even vehicles from our division motor pool.

When we were approximately two kilometers east of the city limits, I suggested to my commanding officer that I take a small squad from my First Platoon and proceed forward from the main body of our column to reconnoiter our front and flanks in order to prevent any possible enemy ambush. Colonel Eason quickly agreed. I then immediately ordered three jeeps forward, selected three drivers, a radio operator with an SCR300 radio for communications, and nine men with automatic weapons. I also armed each jeep with a 50-caliber machine gun. We were on our way.

After we had proceeded well ahead of our advancing unit of troops, I noticed a barracks-like structure in the distance on the opposite side of the road. A uniformed German sentry, armed with an automatic weapon slung across his shoulder, was guarding it. He seemed to be completely oblivious to our presence. I quickly halted our party. We all took cover behind a stone wall fence and waited, fully prepared for a firefight. Amazingly, there was no reaction from the German sentry.

On our side of the road and close to the barracks building, a German haus-frau was hanging out her wash to dry. I signaled her over and asked her if she knew anything about the barracks and its occupants. She told me that it was a German Officer's Training School and that classes were presently in session. I told her that I was sent by General Patton to negotiate the surrender of the men in the barracks or our tanks would blow them all to hell. She seemed to understand and quickly ran across the street to deliver my ultimatum.

She returned shortly and informed me that the German commandant was a senior field officer in the German Army and would not surrender to any officer of a lesser rank. I told her that I was an American colonel and that he had only five more minutes to decide and that I was already in radio contact with Patton's tanks.

She went back to the barracks and delivered my message. To our amazement, she returned with the school commandant followed by fifty young German officer trainees. As they walked out of the barracks building, they placed their rifles and other weapons on a pile and then their commandant presented me with his Luger pistol in a most formal and elegant manner. I asked him where his commanding officer and staff were located. He pointed to a small schoolhouse in the distance. I then set him up on the hood of my jeep and we quickly sped off to the schoolhouse. When we arrived, we jumped out, threw open the doors and I let out a burst from my burp gun over the heads of a group of startled officers and cooks who were just sitting down to a chicken dinner. I accepted their instant surrender. They actually seemed relieved that it was now all over for them.

By this time, the main body of troops that we had left behind had begun to arrive. They were all shocked to see fifty plus German soldiers plus their headquarters staff standing on the side of the road with their hands over their heads. They had a difficult time understanding how a squad of nine GI's could possibly capture so many prisoners at one time and with no bloodshed.

The location of the schoolhouse where this event took place was in a rural area with a mixture of farmhouses and light industry that included medium and

One Soldier's Journey

large manufacturing plants. After our prisoners had been lined up alongside the road, out from these factories slowly drifted a few men and women quickly followed by fifty or sixty more workers. I soon discovered that these people were an assortment of Russian civilians who had been captured by the Germans on the eastern front and then deported to the west to be used as slave laborers. Once the factory workers understood the situation, that they had been liberated and that the enemy was standing in front of them, prisoners under guard, they began to jeer and mock them. I was afraid that they were about to attack the Germans.

One of the factory workers stepped forward, tapped me on the shoulder, bent down, pulled grass and weeds from the ground and began chewing them while indicating to me that this was the only food they had to eat for several days. I noticed that the workers were all extremely emaciated and on the verge of starvation. Immediately, I ordered the German prisoners to remove the rucksacks from their shoulders and place them open on the ground in front of their formation. Out rolled rations of all descriptions. Sausages, breads, biscuits, canned meats, sardines, cheeses, and even a bottle or two of schnapps, were exposed. A mob scene quickly developed and a feeding frenzy of pathetic proportions resulted. At first it was difficult to control the starving bodies as they frantically foraged for food. With aid from our main body of troops, order was quickly restored and a fair and equal distribution of rations was made among the starving workers. Many of them approached me with thankful tears in their eyes for they now seemed to realize that the generous and caring Americans had finally liberated them.

The objective of the Ninth Army, however, had not yet been realized. Consequently, the 79th Division was again earmarked for a pivotal role. The Ninth Army was to close up the Ruhr River pocket and then wait for the arrival of the 1st Army units pushing up from the south. Once the 1st Army came onto the scene, the 79th was then to break across the Kanal and drive into the Ruhr valley.

On 7 April, we advanced across the Kanal and captured Gelsenkirchen, Oberhausen, Dinslaken, Buttop and Gladbeack in the face of scattered resistance. Two days later, we reached our objective, the north bank of the Ruhr River. After that, we cleared the industrial cities of Bochum and Mulheim. On 16 April, our encirclement was complete. We held the banks of the Ruhr River. At this point, the 79th Division lost contact with the enemy in the European Theater of Operations. The next day, 17 April 1945, we learned that our Commander-in-Chief, Franklin Delano Roosevelt, had died on April 12th. It was a sad day for us all. President Roosevelt would not be alive to relish the unconditional surrender of the Germans.

Chapter 36

Mayor of Bochum

Bochum, Germany
April 17, 1945 – April 21, 1945

After our encirclement of the Ruhr Valley and the industrial cities of Bochum and Mulheim, thousands of enemy troops began to surrender, along with many civilian government office holders who were sympathetic to the Nazi cause. Germany was in turmoil and the re-establishment of order was placed on emergency status. The rapid advance of the Russian army that was closing in fast to capture the city of Berlin compounded this endeavor. Rumors were running rampant and the consensus was that Hitler and his staff were fleeing to his redoubt in the Austrian Alps with an army of soldiers labeled, "werewolves." They pledged to fight until the death to defend Hitler and the Third Reich.

There was a Civil Affairs Battalion in the military whose mission was to establish civilian order in areas that had been previously captured by the Allies. Before they arrived, I was given the temporary assignment of taking over control. Bochum had a population of a quarter million, was highly industrialized and had contributed greatly to Germany's war effort. Our main job was to spread motorized patrols throughout the city to prevent looting and to disperse large groups of civilians who might erupt into rebellious crowds and pose a threat to our GI's.

When we entered the city, each one of my four platoons appropriated, better described as "commandeered," any large unoccupied building or private home as temporary living quarters. At this point, the Germans were exceedingly cooperative and surrendered their homes to our troops without any complaints. This was a terrifying experience for many of the German families who were not members of the Nazi party and who had sick or infirm members in their households. They were literally booted out of their homes.

I established my command post, which included my headquarters staff, in the mayor's office in the City Hall. I established telephone communications with each platoon leader along with both radio and telephone contact with battalion headquarters.

Since we were now operating in a non-combat mode, we began to receive orders from headquarters on how to properly conduct ourselves as we interacted with the German civilians in order to make a good impression upon them. Fatigue clothes were out, olive drab class A uniforms were in along with polished boots and neckties. Our living quarters were to be inspected, unannounced, every other day. Strict discipline among the men was also to be exercised. While trying to maintain an element of decorum, we were also functioning as a motorized police force subtly warning the Germans that we would not tolerate any enemy misbehavior. Although an armistice or surrender had not yet been declared, both the Allies and the Germans knew that it was "all over." Only the papers remained to be signed.

On the third day after my platoons had settled into their new quarters, First Sergeant John Haines from Des Moines, Iowa, and I decided to hold an impromptu, unannounced inspection of each platoon's residential quarters. We entered the first house and upon the cry of "Attention" from Sergeant Haines, we proceeded to check each room for neatness and order. As we were leaving one of the bedrooms, Sergeant Haines said, "Good God, Lieutenant, didn't you see that soldier in bed with a woman?" I replied, "No, Sergeant, I was checking for neatness and order, not soldiers in bed with women." Of course, I did see them, and I could have sworn that the young lady was one of those slave laborers that we had rescued outside of Essen. I then realized that she probably had been traveling with us ever since we left Essen, dressed in GI clothes and protected as the platoon's resident prostitute. I dismissed this episode, having more serious concerns to cope with, although I smiled inwardly knowing that one could never underestimate the American soldier and his ability to improvise even in the sex department during times of war.

One Soldier's Journey

On the fourth day of our occupation while I was still serving as "Mayor of Bochum," a German housewife came to my office in tears. She complained that one of my soldiers had stolen her purse that had contained all of her ration coupons plus about seventy-five German marks. I instructed Sergeant Haines to contact each platoon leader and order a collection be taken up to replace the stolen marks. A little over four hundred marks were gathered up. I then told Sergeant Haines to take the lady down into the basement of City Hall where there was a large cabinet filled with ration books. I instructed him to give her three books that contained coupons for scarce food, clothing and other staples.

Within an hour of that episode, I looked outside my large office window and saw a group of people beginning to form a line outside of the City Hall building where Sergeant Haines, myself and those damnable ration books were stored. How fast news spread! Outside about two hundred people were clamoring for ration books. Sergeant Haines and I dispensed them all to show how generous we Americans could be. I also did not want a revolt on our hands.

I did not receive any medals from the Army for this act of charity but received a real chewing out from the Civil Affairs people who were starting to take over my job. We apparently disrupted the entire local economy by our action. Later, Sergeant Haines and I had a real chuckle over our apparent faux pas with those ration books.

Mid-morning April 17, 1945, by special messenger to my headquarters in Bochum, I received an order that came as a completely, unexpected surprise to me. It was Special Order Number 98, Headquarters, 79th Division, APO 79, U.S. Army. It was dated April 19, 1945. Paragraph 6 of the order stated:

> **O's and Em's listed below, org indicated are placed on TD[20] to the Reception Sta in the US under which their name are listed for forty-five (45) days rest and recuperation, addresses shown, and will proceed to the 18th Ref Depot rptg upon arrival to the CO thereof on the 20 April 1945 for tranp. Correspondents and publishers will be notified to discontinue mailing letters and publications until they receive notification of new address. V-mail notice to correspondents and publishers, WD AGO form 971-1, 9**

---

[20] Temporary Duty.

Oct 1943 may be used for that purpose. Information concerning War Department, Army or personnel of a military nature within the theater will not be discussed in private or public and will not be disclosed by means of newspapers, magazines, book lectures or radio, or any other method without clearance through the War.

Department Bureau of Public Relations or the appropriate Public Relations Office of army installations. Travel by military, naval, or commercial aircraft, belligerent vessel, rail or motor transportation is authorized. Ea individual listed accepts this privilege with the definite understanding that he is to be returned to the same overseas command upon completion to his TD in the US. Authorization: VOCG 9th Army Command.
    1st LT. JAMES L. THOME, 01313514, 315TH INF, REGIMENT
    Grand Rapids, Michigan

As my shock subsided, I came to the realization that I had survived the war and I was going home, at least for forty-five days. I doubted very much whether I would return to my beloved Company L because the war was now over and my next stop would probably be Japan.

That evening, after dinner and after our bugler sounded the end of day, I called for a company formation in the Village Square. There, I bid my men all an emotional goodbye. I didn't notice too many dry eyes among the 152 brave, loyal and dedicated soldiers from my Company L.

Chapter 37

Camp Lucky Strike and Homeward Bound

Le Havre, France to Camp Patrick Henry – Newport Beach, Virginia
April 22, 1945 – May 8, 1945

    An aura of calmness had descended upon the civilian population of Bochum even though a few sporadic rifle shots could still be heard in the distance. Perhaps the townsfolk began to realize that their long struggle would soon be over and that normalcy would once again return to their lives. Children were again playing in the streets while the women and old men had begun sweeping and cleaning up the remnants of war.
    We all knew that the war was finally over when Mussolini, the Italian dictator, was captured and shot on 28 April, and when two days later, Hitler committed suicide in his bunker under Berlin. Hitler and his loyal "werewolves" never made it to his redoubt in the Austrian Alps.
    When I had received orders for my rotation furlough, I had the opportunity to select one enlisted man from my Company to go with me. Without hesitation, I choose Private First Class Bob Calcatera who worked as a messenger and radio operator in my company headquarters unit. Bob was a wonderful, non complaining and loyal GI from Herrin, Illinois, who was drafted. Like me, he had more combat time on the front lines than any other soldier in our regiment. We both had learned how to survive through our experiences in the Normandy hedgerows. Bob was overwhelmed when I informed him that I

had selected him to accompany me. Without hesitation, he quickly agreed to come along. I could not have made a better choice. He never let me forget that I was once a private too. Many times I wanted to promote him to a corporal or even to a sergeant. He always refused and told me that he would rather be a first class private then a second class corporal. I told him that I too would rather be a first class lieutenant than a second class captain.

The morning after my emotional "good-bye" to Company L, I contacted our regimental service company to make arrangements to retrieve my meager possessions from where they had been stored while I was in Europe. I then hastily gathered my belongings and stuffed them into my barracks bag in hurried preparation for my departure home. As I prepared to leave Bochum, I was given the assignment to deliver twelve other senior non-commissioned officers to an assembly point outside of Dortmund. I collected up my traveling companions and from that point we were transported by army vehicles through the German and French countryside, devastated and destroyed by the ravages of war, to the French port of Le Havre.

Outside of Le Harve was an army base called Camp Lucky Strike. It was a large, sprawling military installation used as an assembly and staging area for GI's returning home from the war front as a result of furloughs, either medical or rotation, and for other reasons as well. The base was a beehive of activity. Individual soldiers and complete units were being processed, along with the necessary paperwork, for shipment home.

Shortly after we arrived at Camp Lucky Strike, I was walking near the officer's quarters when I heard the cry of, "Hey, Thome!" I turned around and there stood Lieutenant "Pattock," the same young officer I had arrested for being intoxicated back in December when we were attacking the Siegfried Line. I can't describe a more humble man. He profusely thanked me again and again for arresting him. He insisted over and over again that through my action back in December, I had saved his life. Although he had been reclassified and was now in the Transportation Corps, it was apparent that he had connections with the Quartermaster Corps. In no time, he furnished me with a jeep for personal use, a complete new uniform and anything else I needed, including a brand new, soft leather, rare, and much desired pair of paratrooper boots. When I walked up that gangplank and departed from Le Havre, I left in style thanks to Lieutenant "Pattock."

One Soldier's Journey

Our sailing date from France was May 3, 1945. As I stood on the after deck of our Liberty troop transport, I could hardly believe that France was slowly disappearing into the mist of the English Channel. This was a moment in time filled with relief and hopeful expectation. All ears aboard ship were directed toward the ship's loud speakers waiting for the captain to announce that the war had ended and an armistice declared.

On May 8, 1945, while we were in mid-ocean, Victory in Europe was announced over our loud speakers by the ship's captain followed by several blasts from the ship's foghorns. I did not detect any exuberance or happy celebrations among those on the ship. The news was calmly accepted as though it was expected. There were a few moments of reflective silence as though we were all thinking of what was next to come or perhaps thoughts of what we had all just experienced, a war unlike any other in the history of the world.

The crossing itself was quite uneventful after that, yet interesting because I had the opportunity to really learn how to play bridge, the hard way. On board in the officers' lounge, there was a twenty-four hour bridge marathon constantly in progress. When a participant would get up and leave, another player would quickly fill in. I had the opportunity to play many times with an Italian physician from Brooklyn, a cannon company commander from the 30th Division, and a dentist from the 82nd Airborne Division. These guys were ruthless and unforgiving with their bidding wars. Our kidneys really suffered, inasmuch as if anyone would leave to pee, his seat would be forfeited until another vacancy occurred. Consequently, no one wanted to give up his place at the table until absolutely necessary.

Prior to our departure from France and Germany, we were all warned not to take any scientific equipment with us as souvenirs. The U.S. Government did not want us to deplete Europe of this material. Against all warning, my newfound physician friend from Brooklyn had "liberated" a beautiful and expensive microscope from the Zeiss factory in Germany. He was worried sick that he would be arrested and charged by customs if caught. At our bridge table, the rest of us also continued to warn him about the penalties and consequences that he would suffer if discovered. Time at Fort Leavenworth, the military prison, we told him, was a sure thing. Even our dentist friend had somehow smuggled aboard ship a parachute. He wanted to bring it home to use the material to have a wedding dress made for his daughter. He was also worried about being caught by customs for stealing government equipment.

One Soldier's Journey

Our ship was to dock at Newport News, Virginia. From there we would be processed for our furloughs at Camp Patrick Henry, a short distance from the port. As we were being piloted and tugged into port, my physician friend, sick with fear, reached over the side of the ship and dropped his contraband microscope into the swirling waters of the Atlantic. As it gurgled and sank into the foamy sea, I could detect a tear in his eye. An hour later, the ship's captain declared over the ship's loudspeaker that our ship was declared an "open" ship and that all customs inspections would be waived. In front of me going down the gangplank, I observed my dentist friend, a huge smile on his face, leaving the ship with his parachute bouncing against his butt as my physician friend was cursing in Italian.

Chapter 38

USA!

Camp Patrick Henry – Newport News, Virginia
May 1945

When our ship docked at Newport News, ours was the first troop transport to arrive home from Europe after VE Day. The city went crazy with excitement as they welcomed us home. It was a time for much celebration for everyone. Flags and banners of all description were displayed along the streets of Newport News. As we disembarked, whistles and horns were sounding off throughout the city. Businesses, stores and factories were all shut down and it seemed as if the entire population of Newport News turned out to greet us. We were welcomed home as heroes and many of us finally believed that we really were. Our pride in what we had accomplished and our love for the United States of America was unbounded.

After we left our ship and ran through the gauntlet of enthusiastic civilians standing in a mass at the end of our gangplank, we were quickly ushered into army trucks that were standing by and rapidly transported to Camp Patrick Henry. After our arrival there, we waited for our ship's hold baggage to catch up to us, received medical clearances and completed the paperwork necessary to process us for our final destinations after our scheduled furloughs.

According to army regulations, each soldier eligible for an extended furlough or leave was entitled to free government transportation to the military base nearest his home. It would then be the soldier's responsibility to make his own arrangements to reach his final furlough destination. The nearest military

One Soldier's Journey

base closest to my hometown of Grand Rapids, Michigan, was the Sixth Service Command Post at Fort Sheridan, Illinois, an army base located just north of Chicago.

At the railhead, I was assigned a seat on the last coach of a twelve-car troop train and it was there that I finally realized my remarkable good fortune. As our train rolled through the beautiful countryside, the sprawling farmlands, the green meadows and lush cotton, corn and tobacco fields of Virginia, Ohio, Indiana and Illinois, it was difficult to fully comprehend the beauty of our country and that I had made it home safe. I didn't see evidence of the destructive remnants of war. I didn't see ragged, shoeless little children scrounging for food. I didn't see displaced old men and women refugees frantically searching for some kind of shelter. There weren't any dead or bloated cattle scattered among the pastures nor were there any once beautiful and stately trees defoliated and shattered from artillery or aerial bombardments.

As I stood on the observation deck as our train rolled along, it was difficult not to forget the courageous soldiers I had the honor and privilege of serving with. It was difficult not to remember the young soldier who was denied a furlough so that he could be with his wife and children during her serious surgery and who was later killed. It was hard not to remember the hedgerows of Normandy and the bitter cold nights on the Siegfried Line when I arrested Lieutenant Pattock. I could never forget the horrors of the Foret de Parroy, the destruction of Rittershoffen and the wonderful Wollersheim family in Brunssum.

I could never forget the displaced slave laborers, whom we liberated on the outskirts of Essen. I also wondered if the monsieur ever recovered his tall, silk stovepipe hat. I wondered if Lieutenant Mueller told his children and family how a considerate and decent American officer allowed him to be disguised as an American soldier so that he could go home and visit his family. I wondered about Lieutenant Harold Friess and how he was getting along without his right arm. I thought but for the grace of God that could have been me. Finally, I wondered about the families of the approximately 438 men and officers who were either killed or wounded while they were serving with me in Company L and who I had so desperately tried to protect and care for.

I had received my overseas shipping orders on 12 May 1944. One year later, almost to the day, I was home again having lived through an unbelievable experience that was riddled with horror and sadness yet with a happy ending.

One Soldier's Journey

Along the railroad tracks as twilight descended, farmhouses in the distance began to light up which snapped me back to reality. I wondered, "My God, how could all this have happened, and how did I survive?"

I have no idea how I did survive the war. I cannot describe in words the danger I faced and the risks I took. I always had a fatalistic attitude, I guess, and I always figured that no matter what I did, if my time was up, so be it. Consequently, I exposed myself time and time again to machine gun, mortar and artillery fire. Outside of a few bullet and shrapnel holes in my clothes, I was never even scratched. It was absolutely amazing and unexplainable. I feel very, very lucky to be alive.

Chapter 39

Reassignment

Fort Sheridan – Chicago, Illinois to Fort Sam – Houston, Texas
May 16, 1945 – July 8, 1945

    At Fort Sheridan, Illinois on May 16, 1945, post personnel clerks quickly cut orders in order to expedite my leave. Accordingly, Special Order No. 138, dated May 18, 1945, directed me on the first lap of my long journey home from Europe. Special transportation was provided by the Army that transported several of us in our officer group to the downtown "loop" area of Chicago. From there we would all scatter to our final destinations to participate in our long awaited homecomings.
    State Street, Madison, Wabash and Michigan Avenues were crowded with military personnel from all branches of the service celebrating the announcement of VE day. The sailors from the Great Lakes Naval Training Station were the most festive. The nightclubs, bars and theaters were in full operation as was the Empire Room at the Palmer House. Ted Lewis was making everyone happy at the Hotel Sherman's College Inn, as were the parties at the Bismarck Hotel's Walnut Room. When our leave-bound group of soldiers arrived downtown and we exited from our army vehicle, several knelt down and kissed the pavement. It appeared to be an expression of their love, hope and thankfulness for being home.
    My wife, Marian, met me in Chicago. Before we returned to Grand Rapids we shared a wonderful evening together over a candlelight dinner in the Walnut Room of the Bismarck Hotel listening and dancing to the music of Jan Garber.

One Soldier's Journey

I was extremely flattered by all the attention and respect I received from all the civilians I encountered while in Chicago. It seemed as if they were all fascinated by the combat battle stars, ribbons and citations displayed on my uniform I was determined to make the most of my short furlough home because world peace still seemed quite remote.

Although our efforts in the South Pacific were progressing rapidly under the Army's General MacArthur and under the Navy's Admiral Halsey, we all expected that it would be necessary to invade Japan in order to ultimately win the war. My leave orders specified that on June 19, 1945 I was to return to Fort Sheridan for reassignment. I anticipated that I would be assigned to a combat unit scheduled to assist an invasion of Japan. It was made quite clear to me that because hostilities in Europe had ended, I would not be returning to Company L and to the courageous GI's I had left behind.

A round of parties, reunions and dinner engagements greeted my wife and me upon our return from Chicago. Those took up most of my leave time, along with frequent visits to the beaches of Lake Michigan. An elderly great aunt had made her 1941 Dodge sedan available to us and with my military credentials, the gasoline shortage did not present a problem. Between visits to friends and relatives, many long trips to the country were also enjoyed while we made plans for our future. During this period, I found time to visit the Van Dyk family and tell them about the tragic death of their son, Bill. As I said before, the family appreciated my visit and listened to the story of their courageous son with calm dignity.

I reported back to Fort Sheridan, as ordered, on the appointed day of June 19, 1945, and I was promptly handed the following Special Order #172 dated June 20, 1945.

Par, 43. Fol Officers, Groups indicated, having completed a period of TDY this station, are reld atchmt Reception Station #7 and from asgmt organizations and will proceed o/a 20 June 1945 to AGSF REDISTRIBUTION STATION, FORT SAM HOUSTON, TEXAS FOR PROCESSING AND REASGMT. BY COMMAND OF BRIG. GENERAL PIERCE.
1ST LIEUTENANT JAMES L. THOME, INF. 01313514.

One Soldier's Journey

I gathered up my belongings and equipment and along with fourteen other combat officers from the European Theater boarded a military train for the long and monotonous rail trip to Houston, Texas. We were all anxious to discover what the Army had in store for us and what our next assigned station would be.

The post personnel at Fort Sam were all exceedingly friendly and our reassignment officers seemed to be very cooperative and extended every courtesy possible. In turn, we too were friendly, cooperative and courteous to our reassignment officers inasmuch as we weren't too anxious to wind up invading Japan. During my interviews, I was told that due to my combat experience, my citations and decorations, I would undoubtedly be sent to some army station closest to my home so that the Army could exhibit me for public relations purposes. My job would be to make War Bond speeches and visit recruiting stations. Surprises were yet to come.

I didn't have too long to wait for my new assignment and instead of being transferred to an army base closest to my home, I received the following orders:

> **ARMY SERVICE FORCES Army Ground and Service Forces Redistribution Center Fort Sam Houston, Texas 4 July 1945 SPECIAL ORDERS NO. 180, paragraph 53. 1ST LIEUTENANT JAMES L. THOME 01313514, Infantry is reld fr atchd unasg this sta and WP IRTC Cp Blanding, FLA o/a 6 July 45 reporting upon arrival to the CG not later than 22 July 45. (TPA utilized and ten (10) days delay enroute for asgmt and dy EDMCR 9 July 45.**

The order came as a complete shock to me in view of the interviews I previously had with the reassignment officers. Florida certainly was not the nearest post to my home in Michigan, and Blanding could not have been more remote in both distance and isolation. Once an army order was published it was useless to try to have it changed unless there was a serious reason. So, I accepted my new orders and ultimately realized it could have been much worse in as much as the Japanese problem was still a real threat.

I was informed that Camp Blanding was still classified as an Infantry Basic Training Center. I was chosen to instruct new recruits on "how we did it in Europe and how I survived doing it." Most of the young inductees needed

One Soldier's Journey

training as replacement troops in the event we invaded Japan, which was now on the Joint Chiefs' schedule. It appeared to me that the Army was looking for decorated combat veterans to train new recruits in order to maintain the esprit-de-corps and enthusiasm of the infantry soldier. I was supposed to be one of the lucky veterans selected for the job.

Chapter 40

Atom Bomb!

Camp Blanding – Jacksonville, Florida
July 18, 1945 – September 16, 1945

    After I had received my reassignment orders, I had called my home in Michigan and suggested to my wife that if she and my father could somehow purchase a reliable used automobile, she could drive south and we could meet in St. Louis. We could then continue together down to Florida and Camp Blanding.

    Due to the war effort, new automobiles were no longer being manufactured. A relatively good used car would be almost impossible to locate. Against all odds, my father and my wife located a 1937 Ford Deluxe sedan, which she purchased. On July 1, 1945, my wife, accompanied by her brother, drove to St. Louis where we met at the railroad station. There I purchased a railroad ticket for her brother and dispatched him back home to Michigan.

    Marian and I thoroughly enjoyed our ten-day motor trip to our new home in Florida. We spent many enjoyable hours leisurely exploring Mammoth Cave, Cumberland Falls, Gatlinburg and the Smoky Mountains. After we arrived in Florida, we decided that since officer's quarters were unavailable on the post, Gainesville would be a good location to set up housekeeping. It was only about thirty-five miles from the main gate at Camp Blanding, a convenient commute. Also, the Army would partially reimburse me rent money and, in spite of the gasoline and tire shortage, I had a Class A ration card that gave me unlimited quantities of those scarce items.

One Soldier's Journey

After we arrived in Gainesville, we quickly located a newly furnished, five-room bungalow that was being rented out by the fiancée of a soldier who was still overseas. I could leave at 0500 each morning for Camp Blanding and would be able to return home every night except when I took my turn at being battalion Duty Officer or company Duty Officer. Since automobiles were so scarce on base, I usually enjoyed the company of other soldiers who hitched rides with me at the end of the day to their homes outside of camp.

The only difficulty with my daily commute occurred during early morning travel. At that time, the State of Florida had an open range policy among the cattle ranchers. This meant that fencing was not required to contain Florida's large herds of cattle, which were especially prevalent in our area. As a result, cows would sleep on the warm pavement, which made the early morning commute to Camp Blanding like driving an obstacle course. Luckily, I never had an accident.

At Camp Blanding, I was assigned to Company D, 66th Infantry Training Regiment as a platoon leader. It turned out to be a most enjoyable experience. The new trainees were in the midst of their eight-week training cycle and I fit in superbly. I was able to assist them with rifle marksmanship, bayonet and gas warfare training exercises. Each hour of instruction was usually followed by a ten-minute break. During those breaks, I was usually surrounded by the eager young trainees in my platoon who were most anxious for me to relate my combat experiences and any suggestions I might have for their survival. I soon became the most popular officer in my regiment and I was frequently called upon to describe how a particular combat problem was solved.

As the days wore on, I soon became dismayed with my discovery of the poor caliber officer cadre who staffed the Camp Blanding Training Post. With very few exceptions, most of the officers were a smug, self-centered group of individuals. With their constant preening at the Officer's Club while showing off their Good Conduct Medals on their Class A uniforms, they seemed to concern themselves only with protecting their world of polished brass, polished boots and PX privileges along with their own self promotion. Most of them were not qualified for combat and most avoided overseas assignments by appealing to their chaplains, some medical officer for a medical exemption or to a favorite politician. They were excessively protective of their closely guarded society and any stranger was considered a threat to their fantasy world. They resented my popularity among the trainees. I was looked upon as some kind of an alien force

One Soldier's Journey

disrupting the status quo and rocking their boat. All of this was extremely amusing to me. I reacted to this situation by being especially congenial towards all of the officers, cooperative in every way, which infuriated them even more.

Later in July, I was given the assignment to teach young second lieutenants combat tactics as I experienced them while fighting in Europe. Many of these young officers were newly commissioned from college ROTC programs, some were West Point graduates and others were graduates from the Infantry School at Fort Benning, Georgia. Classes were held daily and were generally two-hour sessions. I covered infiltration behind enemy lines, the use of demolitions, small unit (squad, platoon, and company) tactics and how to handle hostile civilian situations with emphasis placed on how to deal with proper ration book distribution.

The month of July went by swiftly. The students in my classes were unusually attentive. Each officer present was convinced without a doubt that he was destined to participate in the invasion of Japan. Every word I spoke was duly noted and I never had to admonish any one of them to "Pay attention!"

The morning of August 6 was warm and bright as my class of about 40 students was gathered beneath the shade of several large live oak trees. I had all of my visual training aids and charts assembled along with a large sand table that I used to demonstrate examples of troop deployment during actual battles in which I had participated. Thus, the stage was set when a jeep drove up and stopped next to my training area.

A colonel from Post Headquarters sat rigidly in the vehicle. I immediately approached him, saluted, and presented him with my lesson plan for the day's instructions. It was the custom, indeed the requirement, that whenever a superior officer approached a teaching site, he must immediately be presented with a lesson plan by the instructor in charge who would have to identify the subject material being taught and the manner in which it was being presented. This inspection procedure, of course, guaranteed that the instructor was prepared and conformed to the training schedules as prescribed by the Army's Plans and Training Program. Instead of accepting my lesson plan, however, the colonel quietly told me the most startling news. I was completely shocked, yet pleased. I wondered, "What now?"

Colonel Adams had called me aside and informed me that on this day, August 6, 1945, the United States Army Air Corps had dropped a super bomb on

One Soldier's Journey
Japan and that by all available accounts, it had completely obliterated the city of Hiroshima and most of its population. An ultimatum was now being prepared by the War Department for the complete and unconditional surrender of Japan. He also told me that in his estimation the war would be over in less than two weeks. It was only a matter of days before we would all be home. He also said that according to rumors from Washington, Nagasaki was next on the list if Japan hesitated.

      The Colonel and I both agreed that since I was only approximately fifteen minutes into my two-hour class period that this information would need to be withheld until my class ended or I would be sure to lose control of the men. Our assumptions were correct. At the end of the first hour, when I told the men what the colonel had said, absolute bedlam broke out among the class. After our ten-minute break, I still had another hour of instructions scheduled. It was obvious that I could not continue. The class was totally disinterested in the subject matter. They were enveloped in joyous celebration. There would be no more killing. They were convinced of that. The invasion of Japan would be canceled along with their invasion training. We were now all aware that it was only a matter of days before we would all be sent home.

Chapter 41

Back to Michigan

Camp Blanding – Jacksonville, Florida
August 1945 – September 16, 1945

    The training program at Camp Blanding was now in a state of flux and partial disarray due to the announcement of the atomic bomb attack on Japan. Discipline and order were maintained but there were some changes in the behavior of the men. In the evenings, everyone listened more attentively for any war news from the radio commentators. Newspapers quickly disappeared from the PX locations situated throughout the camp. Finally, the news came that we had all been waiting for. On August 14, 1945, Japan announced its willingness to surrender. On September second, the official ceremony was held onboard the *U.S.S. Missouri* battleship. Our country was at peace again.
    Our camp activities now became mundane and consisted primarily of the cleaning and care of our military equipment along with various housekeeping chores in and around our barracks area. Rumors were rampant over the presumed deactivation of the military.
    Gossip that was leaking from the Pentagon indicated that a point system was being established in order to accommodate a fair and orderly discharge of our armed forces personnel. It was intimated that each person would receive one credit point for each month served in the United States, two credit points for each month spent overseas and five credit points for each medal awarded for heroic action against the enemy. I quickly totaled up my credit points and

One Soldier's Journey

discovered that I had far in excess of the twenty-five credit points required for immediate discharge.

Within a few days, this point system was confirmed. As I suspected, due to my high credit point score, I was to present myself immediately to our Base Headquarters for deactivation processing. Part of the procedure included a final physical examination before I could be released from active duty. The speed in which these ensuing events unfolded amongst the whirlwind of activity surrounding our camp was difficult to comprehend. The Army bureaucracy just didn't work that way. Nevertheless, on September 15, 1945, I received the following order:

ARMY SERVICE FORCES, Fourth Service Command, Camp Blanding, Florida. Special Orders No. 219. 15 September 1945. Paragraph 12

The following named Officer is reld from organizations indicated this sta, WP to their homes for relief from ACTIVE DUTY, with TDY enroute at Separation Center, Camp Blanding, Florida (reporting to the CO thereat) on 16 September 1945 as required for processing. EDCMR: 23 Sep 45.

1st LIEUTENANT JAMES L. THOME, INFANTRY 01313514

Although my termination from actual active duty was in mid-September 1945, due to accumulated leave time, my formal discharge was dated November 11, 1945. Consequently, I received all pay and allowances due me up to the November date. (Following this, I would, however, be obligated to serve eight years in the Army Reserves, being discharged finally as a Captain, April 1, 1953.)

After I completed all the required paperwork for my discharge from the U.S. Army and passed the exit physical, with mixed emotions and profound sadness, yet with the joyful expectations of my future, I drove our Ford Deluxe sedan to the main gate of Camp Blanding. I stopped there, got out of the car and faced the flag that flew over the main gate. It was there that I gave my final salute and bid "goodbye" to the most unbelievable experience of my life. I then drove back to Gainesville, packed our belongings into the car and drove back to Michigan to the rousing civilian homecoming that lay in wait.

APPENDIX A

Military Vitae

James L. Thome
Captain, Infantry, Army of the United States

Company C, First Battalion, 253rd Infantry Regiment, 63rd Division -
Camp Blanding, Florida and Camp Van Dorn, Mississippi

Company L, Third Battalion, 315th Infantry Regiment, 79th Division -
European Theater of Operations (ETO)

Service:
Entered U.S. Army as a draftee, January 30, 1942
Honorably discharged, Captain, Infantry, April 1, 1953
(Note that I was discharged from the Army as an enlisted man on February 28, 1943, then commissioned as an officer on March 1, 1943. After being relieved of active duty November 11, 1945, I remained in the Reserves until April 1, 1953.)

Service Schools:
Infantry Officer's Candidate School, Fort Benning, Georgia

Assignments:
Platoon Leader, Executive Officer, Infantry Company Commander, Instructor U.S. Ranger School, United States European Theater of Operations.

Service Medals and Decorations:
Good Conduct Medal
American Campaign Medal
WW II Victory Medal
Distinguished Unit Badge
Combat Infantryman Badge

European-African-Middle Eastern Campaign Ribbon
Croix de Guerre with Palm
Honorable Service Lapel Button WWII

Presidential Unit Citation - Third Battalion, 315th Infantry Regiment - Combat Operation in the vicinity of Rittershoffen, Alsace, France January 9, 1945 to January 20, 1945. Awarded July 12, 1945.

4 Bronze Battle Stars for Normandy, Northern France, Central Europe and Rhineland Campaigns.

Bronze Star Medal - Meritorious Achievement in Ground Operations against the enemy, European Theater of Operations, September 14, 1944, Battle at Remois, France. Authorized February 4, 1945. Awarded June 29, 1949.

Bronze Star Medal First Oak Leaf Cluster - Meritorious Achievement in Ground Operations Against the Enemy, European Theater of Operations, Battle in Rittershoffen, Germany, January 11, 1945 - January 20, 1945. Authorized February 4, 1945. Awarded June 29, 1949.

Bronze Star Medal Second Oak Leaf Cluster - Based on the Combat Infantryman Badge for participating in the battles of Normandy, Northern France, Central Europe and the Rhineland. Dates unavailable.

Croix de Guerre with Palm – The Republic of France awarded this citation to the 79th Infantry Division and to the 315th Infantry Regiment respectively and mentioned Monsieur James Thome individually for participation in all their activities as cited in this award.

Letters of Commendation:
Lieutenant Colonel Marion W. Schewe, Headquarters 253rd Infantry Regiment.
General Jacob L. Devers, Headquarters, Army Ground Forces.
Major General Frank L. Culin, Infantry Replacement Training Center (IRTC), Camp Blanding, Florida.

Served Under:
63rd Infantry Division: Major General Louis B. Hibbs
79th Infantry Division: Major General Ira T. Wyche

Other Statistics:
Began Active Duty as an officer	March 1, 1943
Entered Combat	June 19, 1944
Days of Combat	248 Days
79th Division loss of men	23,457
Discharged from Active Duty	November 11, 1945
Continental Service	1 Year, 8 Months, 7 days
Foreign Service	1 Year

APPENDIX B

Second Lieutenant James Leo Thome, fresh out of Officer Candidate School

IMMUNIZATION REGISTER
AND OTHER MEDICAL DATA
(SEE AR 40-210)

NAME: Thome, James L.
ASN: O-1313514
DATE OF BIRTH: Sept 23, 19
RACE: W
BLOOD GROUP: O

SMALLPOX VACCINE

DATE	TYPE OF REACTION	MED. OFF.
2-5-43		J.J.A.
12-29-43		J.J.A.
4-25-45		M.J.N.

TRIPLE TYPHOID VACCINE / TYPHUS VACCINE

DATES EACH DOSE	MED. OFF.	DATES EACH DOSE	MED. OFF.
2-5-43	J.J.A.	5-4-44	E.A.H.
2-18-43	J.J.A.	5-9-44	E.A.H.
2-23-43	J.J.A.	5-15-44	E.A.H.
12-29-43	J.J.A.	1-6-45	J.R.T.
4-25-45	M.J.N.		

TETANUS TOXOID / CHOLERA VACCINE

DATES EACH DOSE	MED. OFF.	DATES EACH DOSE	MED. OFF.
2-13-42	J.J.A.		
3-5-42	J.J.A.		
3-26-42	J.J.A.		
6-8-43	J.J.A.		
12-29-43	J.J.A.		
5-26-44	M.B.		

YELLOW FEVER VACCINE

DATE	LOT NO.	MED. OFF.
3-11-42	371 1/2cc.	J.J.A.

WD AGO FORM 8-117
15 AUG 1944
This form supersedes WD MD Form 81, 23 Sep 1942, which will not be used after receipt of this revision.

OTHER IMMUNIZATIONS

TYPE	DATE	LOT NO.	AMOUNT	MED. OFF.

SPECTACLES

PLACE OF REFRACTION | DATE | GLASSES RECOMMEND YES ☐ NO ☐

V.A. WITH GLASSES | V.A. WITHOUT GLASSES
OD | OS | OU | OD | OS | OU

SPHERE	CYLINDER	AXIS	PRISM	DEC. BL.
OD.				
OS.				
ADD.				

BIFOCAL SEGMENT | FRAME
HEIGHT | INSET | P.D. | BRIDGE | EYE SIZE | TEMPLE
MM. | MM.

POSITION OF EYEGLASS GAS MASK M-1: | SIZE OF GAS MASK:
COMMERCIAL, TYPE, NO. OF PRS. | EYEGLASS, GAS MASK M-1
DATE ORDERED | DATE ISSUED | DATE ORDERED | DATE ISSUED

DENTURES

TYPE	*	DATES INSERTED IF MADE IN SERVICE
FULL UPPER		
FULL LOWER		
PARTIAL UPPER		
PARTIAL LOWER		

* CHECK IF PRESENT WHEN INDUCTED OR ORDERED TO ACTIVE DUTY

DRUG OR SERUM SENSITIVITY

DRUG OR SERUM	
DATE OF REACTION	
TYPE OF REACTION	
SEVERITY	MED. OFF.

REMARKS:

"A Certified True Copy"
James L. Thome
JAMES L. THOME
1st Lt., Inf.

Shot record for Lt Thome indicating receipt of 19 immunizations. He still carries Yellow Fever antibodies.

James and Marian Thome

79th Infantry Division, "Lorraine Division" (Cross of Lorraine)

63rd Infantry Division, "Blood and Fire"

63ᴰ INFANTRY DIVISION

CERTIFICATE

This is to certify that

2d Lt. James L. Thome, 253d Inf.

has qualified as

RANGER

CLEMENT J. COSS,
1st Lt., Inf.,
Div. Ranger Off.

Ranger Certification, 63rd Infantry Division

Form 10.

WESTERN UNION
T.R. CABLEGRAM
(THE WESTERN UNION TELEGRAPH COMPANY)
(Incorporated in the State of New York, U.S.A., with limited liability).

RECEIVED AT 22 GREAT WINCHESTER STREET, LONDON, E.C.2

MR125 GRAND RPAIDS MICH 1944 AUG 24 AM 10 03 85 38 68

EFM

JAMES L THOME O-1313514
AMDYAC LONDON=

U 1659

SON BORN. LOVING GREETINGS FROM ALL OF US
FAMILY ALL WELL.

Announcement of James Michael Thome's birth received while father James was in combat in Europe.

Rites Held for Baby Son Soldier-Dad Never Saw

Funeral services for James Michael Thome, 5 weeks old, of 657 Turner-av., N. W., who died Saturday in Blodgett hospital, were held at 2 p. m. Monday in St. Mary's church and burial was in Mt. Calvary cemetery.

The child's father, Lt. James L. Thome, is in France and never saw the child.

Surviving besides the parents are the grandparents, Mr. and Mrs. John W. Herrmann and Leo J. Thome, all of Grand Rapids.

Unfortunately, LT Thome never got to see his infant son who died at the age of 5 weeks.

First Lieutenant James L. Thome
Late February 1945
Liege, Belgium
Picture taken before crossing the Rhine River

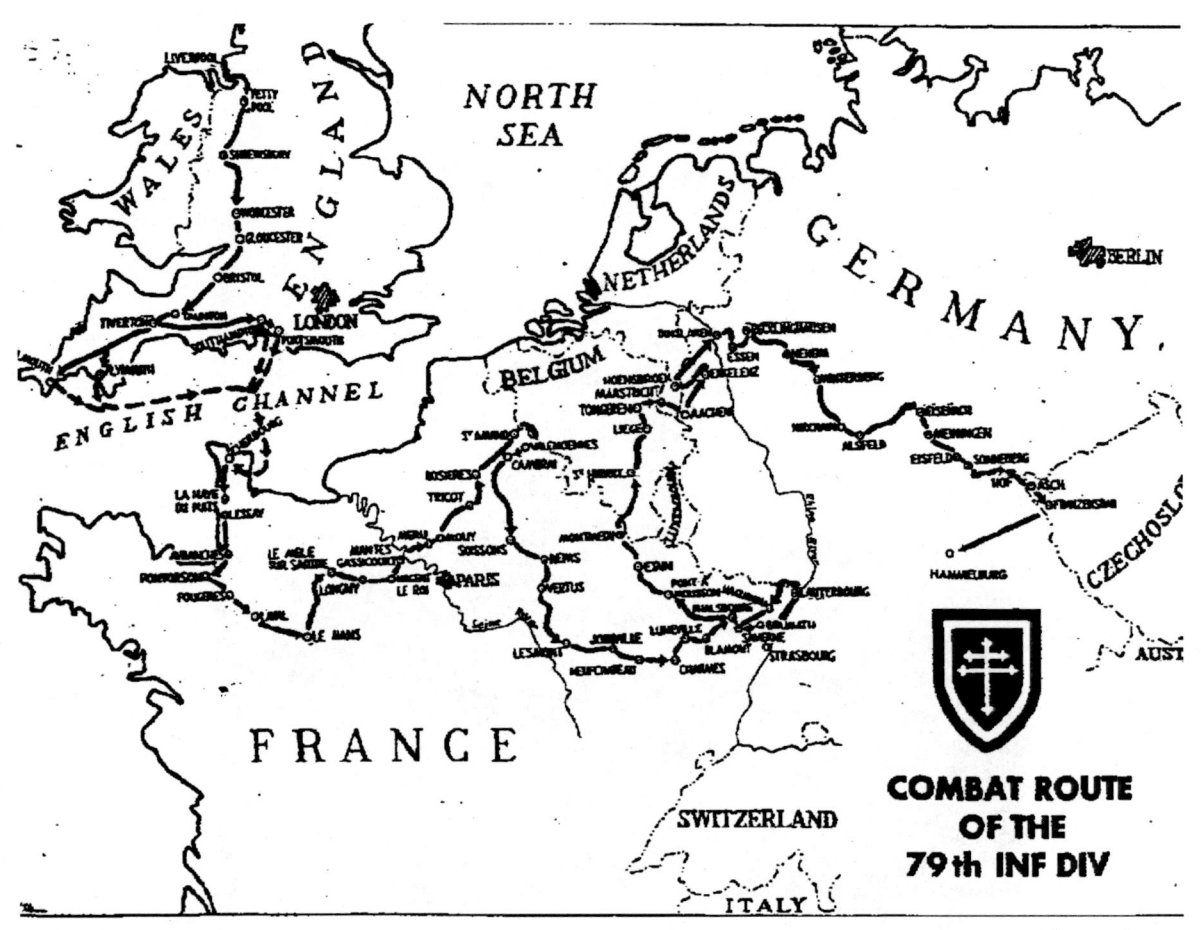

Combat Route of the 79th Infantry Division during World War II. Map courtesy of the 314th Regiment Reunion.

Award of the Bronze Star medal to First Lieutenant James L. Thome

THE UNITED STATES OF AMERICA

TO ALL WHO SHALL SEE THESE PRESENTS, GREETING:

THIS IS TO CERTIFY THAT
THE PRESIDENT OF THE UNITED STATES OF AMERICA
AUTHORIZED BY EXECUTIVE ORDER, FEBRUARY 4, 1944
HAS AWARDED

THE BRONZE STAR MEDAL

TO

First Lieutenant James L. Thome, 01 313 514, Infantry

FOR

MERITORIOUS ACHIEVEMENT
IN GROUND OPERATIONS AGAINST THE ENEMY

European Theater of Operations, 14 September 1944

GIVEN UNDER MY HAND IN THE CITY OF WASHINGTON
THIS 29th DAY OF June 1949

[signature]
MAJOR GENERAL
THE ADJUTANT GENERAL

[signature]
SECRETARY OF WAR

Bronze Star First Oak Leaf Cluster awarded to First Lieutenant James L. Thome

THE UNITED STATES OF AMERICA

TO ALL WHO SHALL SEE THESE PRESENTS, GREETING:

THIS IS TO CERTIFY THAT
THE PRESIDENT OF THE UNITED STATES OF AMERICA
AUTHORIZED BY EXECUTIVE ORDER, FEBRUARY 4, 1944
HAS AWARDED

THE BRONZE STAR MEDAL

First Oak Leaf Cluster

TO

First Lieutenant James L. Thome, O1 313 514, Infantry

FOR

MERITORIOUS ACHIEVEMENT
IN GROUND OPERATIONS AGAINST THE ENEMY

European Theater of Operations, 11 January 1945 – 20 January 1945

GIVEN UNDER MY HAND IN THE CITY OF WASHINGTON
THIS 29th DAY OF June 19 49

MAJOR GENERAL
THE ADJUTANT GENERAL

SECRETARY OF ~~WAR~~ THE ARMY

THE REPUBLIC OF FRANCE

CITATION #5

The Minister of National Defense

CITES TO THE ORDER OF THE ARMY

- Band 79th Infantry Division
- Headquarters and Headquarters Battery
- 79th Division Artillery
- Headuarters and Headquarters Company - 79th Infantry Division
- Headquarters Special Troops - 79th Infantry Division
- Military Police Platoon - 79th Infantry Division
- 79th Quartermaster Company - 79th Infantry Division
- 79th Reconnaissance Troop (Mechanized) - 79th Infantry Division
- 79th Signal Company - 79th Infantry Division
- 304th Engineer Combat Battalion - 79th Infantry Division
- 304th Medical Battalion - 79th Infantry Division
- 310th Field Artillery Battalion (105 Howitzer) - 79th Division Artillery
- 311th Field Artillery Battalion (105 Howitzer) - 79th Division Artillery
- 312th Field Artillery Battalion (155 Howitzer) - 79th Division Artillery
- 313th Infantry Regiment - 79th Infantry Division
- 314th Infantry Regiment - 79th Infantry Division
- 315th Infantry Regiment - 79th Infantry Division
- 463rd Antiaircraft Artillery Automatic
  Weapons Battalion (Mobile) - 79th Infantry Division
- 779th Ordnance Light Maintenance Company - 79th Infantry Division
- 813th Tank Destroyer Battalion (Self propelled) - 79th Infantry Division
- 904th Field Artillery Battalion (105 Howitzer) - 79th Division Artillery

"Spendid unit incited by savage vigor, landed in Normandy in June 1944.

Covered itself with glory in the battles of Saint-Lo and at Haye-du-Puits. Participated in the capture of Fougères, Laval and Le Mans, then crossing the Seine at Mantes-Gassicourt, on 19 August 1944, inflicted heavy casualties on the enemy before marching triumphantly into Paris on 27 August 1944.

By its bold actions, contributed largely to the success of the Allied armies and the liberation of Paris.

This citation includes the Croix de Guerre with Palm

Paris, January 14, 1949
Signed: RAMADIER

REPUBLIQUE FRANÇAISE

EXTRAIT DE LA DECISION N° 5

Le Ministre de la Défense Nationale

CITE A L'ORDRE DE L'ARMEE

- Band la 79 th Infantry Division
- Headquarters and Headquarters Battery - - 79 th Division Artillery
- Headquarters and Headquarters Company - 79 th Infantry Division
- Headquarters Special Troops - 79 th Infantry Division
- Military Police Platoon - 79 th Infantry Division
- 79 th Quartermaster Company - 79 th Infantry Division
- 79 th Reconnaissance Troop (Mechanized) - 79 th Infantry Division
- 79 th Signal Company - 79 th Infantry Division
- 304 th Engineer Combat Battalion - 79 th Infantry Division
- 304 th Medical Battalion - 79 th Infantry Division
- 310 th Field Artillery Battalion (105 Howitzer) - 79 th Division Artillery
- 311 th Field Artillery Battalion (105 Howitzer) - 79 th Division Artillery
- 312 th Field Artillery Battalion (155 Howitzer) - 79 th Division Artillery
- 313 Infantry Regiment - 79 th Infantry Division
- 314 th Infantry Regiment - 79 th Infantry Division
- **315 th INFANTRY REGIMENT - 79 th INFANTRY DIVISION**
- 463 d Antiaircraft Artillery Automatic
  Weapons Battalion (Mobile) - 79 th Infantry Division
- 779 th Ordnance Light Maintenance Company - 79° Infantry Division
- 813 th Tank Destroyer Battalion (self propelled) - 79 th Infantry Division
- 904 th Field Artillery Battalion (105 Howitzer) - 79 th Division Artillery

"*Splendide unité animée d'une énergie farouche, débarque en Normandie en juin 1944. Se couvrit de gloire aux combats de Saint-Lo et à La Haye du Puits. Participa à la prise de Fougères, de Laval et du Mans, puis franchissant la Seine à Mantes-Gassicourt le 19 août 1944 infligea de lourdes pertes à l'ennemi avant d'entrer triomphalement à Paris le 27 août 1944.*
Par ses actions audacieuses a largement contribué au succès des Armées Alliées et à la Libération de Paris."

Ces citations comportent l'attribution de la Croix de Guerre 1939-1945 avec palme

Fait à Paris, le 14 janvier 1949
Signé : RAMADIER

- EXTRAIT CERTIFIE CONFORME
Pau, le 28 septembre 2001
le lieutenant-colonel M.F. BENOIST
commandant le bureau central
d'archives administratives militaires

Cette citation collective ne donne pas droit au port, à titre individuel de la Croix de Guerre à Monsieur THOME James

Honorable Discharge

from the Armed Forces of the United States of America

This is to certify that

Captain James Leo Thome, O1 313 514, Infantry - USAR

was Honorably Discharged from the

Army of the United States

on the __1st__ day of __April 1953__ *This certificate is awarded as a testimonial of Honest and Faithful Service*

ANN CUMMINGS
MAJOR, WAC

Honorable Discharge of Captain James Leo Thome

ACROSS ONE MORE RIVER by Joseph Driscoll

The Rhine, the Roer and the Uwer,
The Saar, the Sauer and the Sure,
The Marne, the Seine and the Aisne,
The Meuse, the Maas and the Mayenne,
The Kull, the Nims and the Prum,
The See, the Sarthe and the Somme,
The Seille, the Vire and the Aure,
The Ourcq, ther Orne and the Loire,
The Aire, the Oise and the Eure,
The Ars, the Bar and the Our,
The Vanne, the Seine and the Rhone,
The Mosel, the Moselle and the Madon,
The Meu, the Mainz, the Meurthe,
The Loire, the Rive, the Ourthe,

The Seiche, the Tille, the Mortagne.
The Scheldt, the Suippes, the Viliane.
The Douve, the Yonne, the Vesle,
The Aube, the Allier, the Bresle,
The Blaise, the Omain, the Vaire,
The Ornan, the Argentan, the Cher,
The Ohre, the Oust, the Gay,
The Gian, the Petrusse, the Lessay.
The Odet, the Semmon, the Rance,
The Erft, the Lye, the Nieder France,
The Oder, the Elbe, the Ems,
The Vaus, the Alzette, the Thames

Alway across one more river

*The Stars and Stripes, Saturday, April 7, 1945

APPENDIX C

About the Author

James L. Thome is 83 years old and has five grown children. He has been retired since 1986 from Merck & Company, a pharmaceutical firm, where he was a representative specializing in infectious diseases and hypertension.

While employed by Merck, Mr. Thome spent several years as a legislative agent representing Merck & Company in the Michigan Legislature. As a Merck lobbyist, he was instrumental in assisting the legislature to pass the mandatory Rubella Bill, which mandated the immunization of all children entering kindergarten against German measles. Michigan was the first state to pass this law.

Mr. Thome was born and raised in Grand Rapids, Michigan, where he spent most of his life. He relocated to Winterhaven, Florida, shortly after he retired from Merck & Company. He now resides at Fairfield Glade Resort, Crossville, Tennessee. He may be contacted at jthome@usit.net.

ISBN 155395084-4